Educating Religiously in the Multi-Faith School

Donald Weeren

Detselig Enterprises Limited
Calgary, Alberta

Donald Weeren
Saint Mary's University
Halifax, Nova Scotia

with contributions by
Sid Bentley and **Mildred Burrows**

Canadian Cataloguing in Publication Data

Weeren, Donald J.
  Educating religiously in the multi-faith
school

  Includes bibliographical footnotes.
  ISBN 0-920490-59-X

  1. Religious education – Canada.   2.
Religious education.   I. Title.
  LC408.C2W44 1986   377'.0971   C86-091202-7

© 1986 Detselig Enterprises Limited
P.O. Box G 399
Calgary, Alberta T3A 2G3

SAN 115-0324

Printed in Canada   ISBN 0-920490-59-X

Contents

Acknowledgments

Like every human accomplishment, this book is the product of many minds, hearts and hands. The names that follow, therefore, are representative of a multitude.

I gratefully acknowledge the contributions of: Saint Mary's University, which supported the graduate course which parented the book and supplied research funds through the Senate Research Committee; Owen Ferguson, Frances Forsyth, Karen Greenman, Brian McAdoo and Edmund Smith, who typify the students from whom I have learned; Sid Bentley and Mildred Burrows, pioneers in educating religiously in their schools and generous participants in this effort to disseminate the concept; Sister Sheila Moore, who exemplifies the willing cooperation of those who administer and staff the programs researched; and my wife, Nancy, discerning critic of the manuscript.

In receiving so much from others and in discovering the form and the words to give to the book, I recognized again that our human endeavors are sustained by God, who shares with us his creative power. This gift above all I acknowledge.

1
Orientation

Educating Religiously in the Multi-Faith School is intended to embrace all schools – whether public, separate or private – which have students and teachers with diverse religious identities. Without denying the important historical, legal and attitudinal distinctions among these schooltypes, I believe that the need for and challenge of educating religiously are often similar in all three.

It is possible that, even before reading further, you are prepared to acknowledge the need in principle. You may accept the view that a school committed to the all-round development of students should not limit itself to teaching skills for living: it should also help students to acquire a sense of the fundamental value and purpose of living. Yet you may see the multi-faith character of a school as an impediment to educating religiously. Once a school enters the domain of religion – of deep, personal convictions about why and how life is to be lived – does it not almost inevitably give offense to the beliefs of one or more groups in its population? Is it not more fair and prudent for teachers, administrators and educational policy-makers to leave religious education wholly to other agencies, notably the family and the faith community?

This book seeks to answer such questions, not so much theoretically, as through current examples of multi-faith schools educating religiously in ways which respect religious differences. However, the case studies which constitute the major portion of the book are not left to speak entirely for themselves. I advance some observations which support not every feature but the overall thrust of the programs. You are invited to weigh those observations as you form your own judgment about each program's appropriateness and value.

This chapter deals with contemporary attitudes towards educating religiously and with their historical roots. In Chapter 2, I probe the meaning of "educating religiously" with the aid of other concepts, such as "educating secularly" and "educating morally." Both chapters borrow from the case material, which you will need to examine in its own right.

Let us begin, therefore, with some glimpses of educating religiously as it occurs in multi-faith schools in Canada.

> My [Grade 12] students acquire a basic understanding of how the Bible was written and edited, and many find pleasure in reading it. I recall one parents' night when a mother's remark, "We could never get our children interested in the Bible, but now I see Allan often reading his, and he

1

seems to enjoy it,'' was followed later that evening by a father's comment, ''When I came home last night, Danny was entertaining his brothers and sisters with a dramatic reading of the description of the leviathan found in the Book of Job.''[1]

* * * * *

Interspersed with some dialogue between teacher and class about recent activities or events, the Grade 1 opening exercises comprised the singing of ''O Canada'' by the children, and the singing of the ''morning song'' with the aid of a tape recorder. The ''morning song'' consisted of morning greetings and of the following prayer:

> Father, we thank Thee for the night
> And for the pleasant morning light,
> For the rest and food and loving care
> And all that makes the day so fair.
>
> Help us do the things we should,
> To be to others kind and good.
> In all we do, in work and play,
> To grow more loving every day.[2]

* * * * *

An elective course on world religions in a British Columbia junior high school attempts to portray a faith ''from the point of view of those who belong to it. . . . This means when I teach Hinduism, 'I am a Hindu,' when I teach Judaism, 'I am a Jew,' and so on. From this base, I support and defend each faith. By emphasizing the positive aspects, I try to present each religion in its ideal form. I do not dwell on the 'darker pages.' Each religion has had its misguided zealots who have done unfortunate things as 'representatives' of that faith.''[3]

* * * * *

The Grade 7 lesson, which began with a review of beliefs and customs regarding birth and death in some pre-industrial societies, dealt with baptism as practiced by various denominations. Students reported on the rite they had undergone, some with much specific detail, even to the point of citing words of the rite. The teacher's role was to supplement the data and encourage reflection, as this exchange illustrates:

Teacher: ''What is the purpose of baptism?''
Student 1:   ''To enter the Kingdom of God.''
Teacher: ''Yes, that is what some people believe.''
Student 2:   ''To give you a name.''
Teacher: ''It is not really necessary for that, because a name can be given when the birth is registered.''[4]

* * * * *

In a Grade 7 lesson on the meaning of some of the Ten Commandments, each of the students was called on individually to answer the question: how do you honor your father and mother? Then the teacher gave a thoroughly realistic rendition of what ''hassling'' or ''saucing'' a parent might sound like. The teacher also turned the searchlight on herself, by sharing with the class some of the details of how she, an adult, attempts to honor her parent.[5]

In each of these instances, students are being educated religiously, an obviously wide-ranging process whose meaning will be explored in Chapter 2. Here, we look at the attitudes behind the process. What set of attitudes makes possible the endeavors described in the case studies and accounts for what is probably the more typical situation in Canadian schools today – the avoidance of educating religiously?

A large body of opinion favors participation by the school in the religious education of young people. In a British Columbia public school, social studies teacher Sid Bentley has found that 95 percent of parents of his students (grade 8/9) give written consent to their taking the optional course on world religions.[6] In a Newfoundland Integrated school board, only 4 percent of students entering grade 10 were "written out" of the religious education course by their parents.[7] Parents of children attending a Nova Scotia suburban public elementary school were asked in a 1983 questionnaire whether religious education should be made part of the elementary curriculum; the response rate was 83.3 percent, and of the respondents 77.7 percent answered the question affirmatively.[8]

The Toronto case study (Chapter 4) is striking evidence of the willingness of widely disparate religious bodies to support a common program of religious opening exercises in public schools. Interviews of clergy in three Nova Scotia communities[9] suggest that religious education courses in public schools would be favored by the major Protestant denominations.

None of these findings can be interpreted as *carte blanche* support of religious education in multi-faith schools; in each instance there are expressed or implied conditions. For example, in one Nova Scotia community the Protestant clergy specified these conditions for public school religious education courses:

1. That material be carefully selected.
2. That instructors be carefully screened.
3. That material be geared to the age of the students.
4. That the program be optional.
5. That the program have no denominational bias.
6. That it promote the Christian ethic.

In another of the communities, respondents felt that clergy should agree on course material. They foresaw problems in that regard, as well as strong objections by a few parents. It is likely that such anticipation of obstacles is itself an obstacle to introducing religious education into public schools.

Opinion against educating religiously in multi-faith schools takes diverse forms. There are those who hold that religion is outside the school's proper domain. K.M. Kryzanowski, past president of the Alberta Teachers' Association, has stated:

I do not see religious studies as a necessary ingredient for a complete education. I believe that the study of religion is a matter which is the prerogative of the home and the church and ought not to be mandated for the public school curriculum.[10]

Ian Bruce Kelsey, President of Canadians United for Separation of Church and State, echoed that statement in registering his objection to religious exercises in schools.

The school is not in the business of teaching or dealing with the divine. The church is. The school deals with a worldly or secular or non-religious sense of things. The church turns the world upside down and views things from a purely spiritual sense of things. If it isn't doing that, it's not doing its job.[11]

Kelsey does, however, recognize the schools' responsibility to educate religiously in one important sense of the term. The argument against school religious exercises

in no way prevents the school from teaching about religion. Our young people need very much to know why particular religious-minded individuals and groups think and act the way they do. Ultimately, study of these religions and their followers will bring greater tolerance, respect and admiration of diverse peoples and diverse religions.[12]

While one body of opinion sees the public school as having no mandate (or only a restricted mandate) to educate religiously, another sees the public school as being unfit for the task. One Pentecostal minister (interviewed in one of the previously mentioned Nova Scotia surveys) held that public school teachers lack the qualifications necessary to teach religion properly. Other judgments are more severe. The public schools are seen as promoters of a self-sufficient humanism, which gives no recognition to the place of God in human affairs.[13] A growing minority of parents has consequently turned away from public schools to support private religious institutions. A noteworthy variant has been the funding of alternative religious schools by the public school board of Calgary, an experiment which has occasioned much controversy, including the 1983 election of seven school board candidates under the "Save Public Education" (SPE) banner, who promised to abolish the religious schools.

In summary, the multi-faith schools in Canada which attempt to educate religiously do so in a climate of opinion which is broadly supportive, but which also comprises highly critical views. Caution seems to be the prevailing sentiment among educators anticipating objections by a minority to religious education initiatives which the majority would accept but not vigorously demand.

The historical roots of these attitudes are worth examining, both to satisfy natural curiosity and to help us determine and evaluate our own attitudes; educational positions taken without consulting the record of human wisdom and error are of doubtful validity.

Starting with one of the earliest school systems for which records exist, that of ancient Sumer, we find that educating religiously was an integral function of the curriculum in the heyday of the Sumerian school, 2500-2000 B.C. The school's principal purpose was the down-to-earth task of training scribes in the use of the intricate Sumerian language and in mathematical skills, for conducting the affairs of a complex society. But the school was also concerned with the general development of its students. The works studied included "myths and epic tales in the form of narrative poems celebrating the deeds and exploits of the Sumerian gods and heroes; hymns to gods and kings; lamentations, that is, poems bewailing the not infrequent destruction of the Sumerian cities; wisdom compositions, including proverbs, fables, and essays."[14] The religious ingredient is evident.

The schools of ancient Greece, direct ancestors of our schools, likewise conveyed a religious interpretation of the universe. When the philosopher Plato (428/7 - 348/7 B.C.) put forward his conception of an ideal educational system, he proposed not an abandonment but a refinement of religious content. The gods should not be depicted as doing evil, contrary to many episodes in the works of Homer and other poets studied by Greek youth. "A poet," wrote Plato, "surely ought always to represent the divine nature as it really is. And the truth is that nature is good and must be described as such."[15] Nor did Plato limit religious education to the study of poetry in the lower stages of schooling. The ultimate learning task for the most gifted individuals, the philosopher-rulers, would be to acquire knowledge of the Good. Plato uses an analogy to describe that supreme reality:

> The Sun not only makes the things we see visible, but also brings them into existence and gives them growth and nourishment; yet he is not the same thing as existence. And so with the objects of knowledge: these derive from the Good not only their power of being known, but their very being and reality; and Goodness is not the same thing as being, but even beyond being, surpassing it in dignity and power.[16]

Rome eventually vanquished Greece and the whole Mediterranean world and much beyond, but the Greek gods were not repudiated in society or in the school. There was "a widespread feeling that to slight the gods, plural, was wrong,"[17] and thus it was not surprising that Greek gods took their place along with other deities in the literary curriculum of the Empire. Describing his education in North Africa centuries after the conquest of Greece, Augustine (354-430) mentioned studying Homer as well as Latin poets whose writings were peopled with gods.

Augustine exemplifies not only the standard scholastic experience of the Roman Empire but also its rejection in favor of a curriculum consonant with the increasingly widespread Christian faith. In the *Confessions* he relates how he was set the task of portraying the goddess Juno in her anger at being unable to prevent Aeneas, the Trojan prince, from going to Latinum:

> We were forced to go astray in the footsteps of these poetic fictions. . . .
> And his speaking was most applauded, in whom the passions of rage and
> grief were most pre-eminent, and clothed in the most fitting language,
> maintaining the dignity of the character. What is it to me, O my true life,
> my God, that my declamation was applauded above so many of my own
> age and class? is not this all smoke and wind? and was there nothing else
> whereon to exercise my wit and tongue? Thy praises, Lord, Thy praises
> might have stayed the yet tender shoot of my heart by the prop of Thy
> Scriptures; so had it not trailed away amid these empty trifles, a defiled
> prey for the fowls of the air.[18]

"The prop of Thy Scriptures" was to become universally available to students in the ensuing centuries. The literature of Rome and Greece would not be expunged from the curriculum – indeed, it would, from the Renaissance to the nineteenth century, again enjoy pre-eminence among secular studies – but it would no longer be regarded as an expression of religious realities. For those, students would turn to the Old and New Testament, the writings of the Fathers of the Church (Augustine being one of them), and Christian catechisms.

That the curriculum of schools should encompass religious content was thus accepted both in antiquity and after the Christian church became ascendant. Medieval and Reformation-era sources indicate that neither church nor home was seen as having exclusive responsibility for the religious education of young people. That function was also expected of the school.

Two figures associated with the genesis of the idea of universal public schooling are worth noting. Martin Luther (1483 - 1546), criticizing existing schools as "unchristian and sensual" in character, urged that the civil authority establish schools "on a more Christian basis," where a person could become qualified "to dispense the word of God and the Sacraments."[19] (Though in this letter to the German mayors and aldermen Luther spoke of the disabilities of families with regard to educating their offspring, it is clear that he conceived of the school in partnership with, rather than supplanting, the home. He saw the *pater familias* as a principal catechist of the church. His "prefaces to the German Mass and to the small and large catechisms insist upon the religious responsibility of fathers to children and servants."[20]

The second figure is the Moravian educator and churchman, John Amos Comenius (1592 - 1670), regarded as a herald of modern, universal schooling. Comenius saw the "Mother School" (i.e., the home) as only the first stage of an education whose aims he described as follows:

> We must . . . concentrate our energies on obtaining that, throughout our
> whole lives, in schools and by the aid of schools: (i) our talents may be
> cultivated by the study of the sciences and of the arts; (ii) languages may

be learned; (iii) honest morals may be formed; (iv) God may be sincerely worshipped.[21]

The notion that the school should abstain from educating religiously is thus a recent one. It emerges prominently only after some four millennia, in the present century, although it was latent in nineteenth-century developments.

The nineteenth century saw the establishment in Europe and North America of universal schooling, funded and controlled by government. How were public educational systems to accommodate cases of religious diversity and, in many instances, disharmony within the population? How was a unitary state to manage the task of education which, since the Reformation, the various denominations had typically performed through their own schools?

Solutions were not easily arrived at, for deep convictions and prejudices about the transmission of life-values to young people were at stake. Eventually, a range of policies emerged, differing in the manner and degree in which the publicly funded school system mirrored the religious divisions of the society. To cite two contrasting examples, in Newfoundland public funding was allocated exclusively to denominationally controlled schools; in British Columbia, public funding was allocated exclusively to non-sectarian public schools, in which "no clergyman of any denomination shall be eligible for the position of Superintendent, Deputy Superintendent, Teacher or Trustee."[22] Even in the latter case, however, the decision not to reflect denominational differences in the structure of the school system did not entail making schools areligious. By law, the Bible was still to be present, in the form of comment-free daily readings, accompanied by the recitation of the Lord's Prayer.[23]

The British Columbia model showed similarities to practices found in the United States until the 1960s. Notwithstanding the already-established separation of church and state in education, twelve states required daily Bible readings by law, another twelve specifically permitted such readings, and another thirteen were silent on the matter, leaving it to the discretion of local school boards. Only eleven states prohibited school Bible reading.[24] About thirty percent of American schools conducted "a morning devotional, usually in the form of the Lord's Prayer."[25] In 1962, however, the Supreme Court ruled that such official devotional exercises tended to coerce religious minorities or non-believers into conforming and conflicted with the constitutional ban on the establishment of religion by the government. A year later, Bible readings were likewise ruled unconstitutional. President Kennedy's observation following the first ruling is illuminating. There was, he said, a remedy for everyone to the ban on prayer in schools, "namely 'to pray ourselves' at home and in church, and to provide religious guidance for 'our children'."[26] The statement summed up the willingness to dispense the school from forms of educating religiously which had once been accepted as proper and necessary. That the willingness was not universal is apparent from continuing efforts in the United States to legitimize school prayer once again.

Some forms of educating religiously in schools were not only upheld but probably fostered by the Supreme Court decisions. Justice Clark, writing the majority opinion in the 1963 decision, said:

> One's education is not complete without a study of comparative religion or the history of religion and its relationship to the advancement of civilization. It certainly may be said that the Bible is worthy of study for its literary and historic qualities. Nothing we have said here indicates that such study of the Bible or of religion, when presented objectively as part of a secular program of education, may not be effected consistent with the first amendment.[27]

The latter half of the twentieth century has been a time of increased religious pluralism, a pluralism that includes the choice to disavow belief in divinity or a supernatural order. Whether juridically, as in the United States, or simply sociologically, as in Canada and several other western societies, the sensitivity to pluralism has prompted reticence and caution with respect to educating religiously in public schools.

Such hesitance also affects non-public schools. They, too, show a diversity of religious outlook among staff and students and raise questions about the continued viability of practices developed at a time of greater religious cohesion – at least greater *overt* cohesion – in their populations.

A good example of this change is provided by the Netherlands, which has been considered a classic case of religious segmentation in publicly funded schooling. The Dutch solution to the nineteenth-century dilemma of how to educationally accommodate the nation's religious diversity was to fund with public money both publicly and privately managed schools. As a result there arose three large systems – Catholic and Protestant (these being privately managed), and public – along with a smaller sector sometimes referred to as "neutral private." Both the Protestant and the Catholic system were committed to educating religiously, in the sense of providing formal religious instruction and a pattern of school life conducive to faith and practice.

Today Dutch Protestant and Catholic schools exhibit a diversity of religious outlook analogous to that of the public schools. For example, a large majority of students in an urban Protestant high school I visited in 1983 could be described as having no active religious affiliation, and there was a significant presence of students of non-Christian origin, exemplified in one class by two practising Moslems and two secularized Moslems. A Catholic study states that "religion classes are taken by many students baptized as Catholics but no longer involved with the church, students without a Catholic background, and students from other religious traditions."[28] In the two Catholic schools I visited, school prayer, a visible feature of Catholic education in the past, is not a standard daily occurrence. The administration of one of the schools recommends that teachers start the day with a Bible reading, prayer, or period of reflection, but not all teachers feel able to do so. The principal remarked that one has to have the courage of one's convictions in order to pray in class, for students at first may exhibit hostility to the practice.

This comment brings us once again to the present. My aim has been to show that current attitudes of support, reticence and opposition towards educating religiously are rooted in the experiences and choices of the past. There is a deep historical foundation – and, I would argue, a sound one – for considering the school as a legitimate and needed partner in religious education. At the same time, there have been historical reasons, not always edifying ones – I cite the record of interdenominational animosity among Christians – for placing the school under greater or lesser restrictions, depending on the educational jurisdiction. The choice open to the public and the educational profession today is: should wider scope be given to the multi-faith school to educate religiously? Or should we expect of the multi-faith school even less than we did in the recent past?

History takes us only so far. It helps us pose the right questions, it may even suggest answers, but it makes no decision for us. To decide wisely on the role of multi-faith schools in religious education, we should consult the experience of our contemporaries. That is what the rest of this book is about, the next chapter suggesting some interpretive categories, and the remaining chapters illustrating how Canadian educators are attempting to educate religiously in multi-faith schools.

Notes

[1] From Chapter 3, "Biblical Literature in the High School," pp. 34-35.

[2] From Chapter 4, "Daily Readings/Prayers: the Toronto Model," pp. 46-47.

[3] From Chapter 7, "A 'Religions of the World' Course for Junior High School Students," p. 83.

[4] From Chapter 5, "Religious Study in the Regular Curriculum," pp. 61-62.

[5] From Chapter 6, "Elective Religious Study in an Elementary/Junior High School, " p. 75.

[6] Chapter 7, p. 81.

[7] Chapter 5, p. 56.

[8] Frances N. Forsyth, "A Survey of Parental Attitudes and Concerns towards Religious Education in the Public Elementary School System," unpublished report, March 31, 1983, p. 4.

[9] Interviews done by my graduate students Brian McAdoo, Karen Greenman and Edmund Smith, and Owen Ferguson, in 1983.

[10] From a talk by K.M. Kryzanowski, reproduced in the Alberta Teachers' Association Religious Studies and Moral Education Council *Newsletter,* Vol. 9, No. 1, August, 1982, p. 7.

[11]Ian Bruce Kelsey, "The Power of Prayer," *Canadian School Executive,* Vol. 1, No. 6, December, 1981, p. 4.

[12]Ibid.

[13]An example of this type of criticism is: Tom Malcolm and Harry Fernhout, *Education and the Public Purpose* (Toronto: Curriculum Development Centre, n.d. [post-1978]).

[14]Samuel Noah Kramer, *The Sumerians* (Chicago: University of Chicago Press, 1963, p. 233. Chicago Press, 1963), p. 233.

[15]Plato, *The Republic,* translated by Francis MacDonald Cornford, paperback (London: Oxford University Press, 1945), II, 378, p. 71.

[16]Ibid., VI, 508, p. 220.

[17]Ramsey MacMullen, *Paganism in the Roman Empire* (New Haven, Conn.: Yale University Press, 1981), p. 2.

[18]*The Confessions of Saint Augustine,* translated by Edward B. Pusey, (New York: Pocket Books, 1951), Book I, p. 16.

[19]Frederick M. Binder, *Education in the History of Western Civilization: Selected Readings* (London: MacMillan Company and Collier-MacMillan, 1970), pp. 160, 164.

[20]William Haugaard, "The Continental Reformation of the Sixteenth Century," in John Westerhoff III and O.C. Edwards, Jr., *A Faithful Church* (Wilton, Connecticut: Morehouse-Barlow, 1981), p. 132.

[21]From the *Great Didactic,* as excerpted in Binder, op. cit., p. 184.

[22]Section 14 of the Consolidated Public School Act, 1876, cited by C.B. Sissons, *Church and State in Canadian Education* (Toronto: Ryerson Press, 1959), p. 381.

[23]Section 167 of the Public School Act, cited in *Religious Education in Schools of Canada* (n.p.: Department of Christian Education, Canadian Council of Churches, n.d. [1963]), p. 19.

[24]Don Conway, "Summary Statement of Legal References Related to Problems of Religion and Public Education," *International Journal of Religious Education,* March, 1956, pp. 36-37.

[25]*New York Times,* July 1, 1962, p. 1E.

[26]Ibid.

[27]Nicholas Piediscalzi, "Religion Studies in Public Education: U.S. Supreme Court Decisions and Recent Developments." Document issued by Public Education Religion Studies Center, Dayton, Ohio, n.d.

[28]Simon van Beurden et al., *Katechese Bestek* (Nijmegen: Hoger Katechetisch Instituut, 1982), p. 9.

2
Exploring the Concepts

The examination of actual cases of educating religiously is the main task which this book sets before you. By way of preparation, this chapter and the preceding one invite you to consider within what frame of reference you will examine the cases. Evidently, one should formulate a frame of reference tentatively rather than definitively. Otherwise, instead of helping one to discover significance in the case material it might lead only to a pre-conceived, distorted reading of the data.

So far I have suggested that your frame of reference include an awareness of the historical basis for current attitudes towards educating religiously in multi-faith schools. Now I am suggesting that it incorporate certain conceptions of what educating religiously means.

My suggestions, it should be noted, take the form of a series of reflections rather than a methodical analysis of the literature on the subject. The theme running through the reflections is that of connectedness: concepts and disciplines may be distinguished intellectually, but they occur together in reality. This phenomenon can be exemplified by brief references to the case studies, presented in chart form on page 12.

It should not surprise us that what stands apart when defined does not do so when observed. A definition is a mental construct necessary for understanding and effectively utilizing the thing defined, but is not a strictly true representation of it. In its true state, the thing exists as an integral part of the tightly and intricately woven fabric of reality. Define it, disentangle it, and we lose some of its meaning, some of its myriad ties with the rest of the real order.

I am arguing, therefore, that the blurring of theoretical distinctions in reality is altogether normal and natural. This should become more apparent as each of these sets of concepts is explored in turn: educating and nurturing; religion and secularity; educating religiously and educating secularly; educating religiously and educating morally; informing and influencing.

Educating and Nurturing

Both educating and nurturing are readily associated with development. To illustrate: we are accustomed to saying that education promotes the *development* of a person's mind, character, physical capacities etc., and that inadequate nurture stunts a person's development.

11

Concepts distinguished in theory	Concepts blended in practice
Literature/Religion	In studying the Bible as literature, one also leans more of the humanity-divinity relationship. (Chapter 3)
The mundane/The spiritual	Example: A teenager's relationship with his/her parents embodies or repudiates religious norms. (Chapter 6, p. 75)
	Example: Conflicts of personality within a family are mirrored in religious data. (Chapter 5, pp. 58-59)
Moral values/Religious values	Example: Unselfishness is seen as a religious quality. (Chapter 6, p. 77)
	Example: Credulousness is indicted as an ultimate evil. (Chapter 4, p.43)
Study of world religions/Personal religious growth	A course on world religions can help a student in the search for answers to existential questions (Chapter 7)
Religious knowledge/ Religious nurture	Example: A course on the sacraments is also an opportunity for students and teacher to share their inner religious feelings, including the teacher's perceptions of why one should participate in worship each week. (Chapter 6, p. 76)
Community building/ Religious exercises	Example: A grade 1 class gathers each morning to share experiences, to greet one another, to sing of their country, to sing of blessings from God and of help from God in being "to others kind and good." (Chapter 4, p. 46)

Development in the present context means becoming fully human, that is, achieving humanity in the widest and deepest ramifications of the term. If we were to spell out those ramifications, we would come up with an extensive catalogue of such descriptors as: material, spiritual; personal, social; physical, intellectual, emotional, moral; creative, conserving; scientific, literary, artistic; religious, secular.

Being educated and being nurtured may be viewed as distinct paths to development. The former connotes learning in deliberate, conscious fashion; the latter connotes imbibing sustenance and support unreflectively. Applied to religious development, the terms have been clearly differentiated in the literature. As explained by one leading religious educator, religious nurture has to do with religious upbringing, with the fostering of a particular faith, whereas religious education has to do with "an open, descriptive, critical, enquiring study of religion."[1]

It can be argued that nurturing is the appropriate function of the home and the faith community (i.e., church, synagogue, mosque, etc.), whereas educating is the appropriate function of the school. Home and faith community are the environment from which one imbibes perceptions of what is worthy and unworthy. They nourish the developing person with words and experiences that delimit an attitude towards life, a way of life. The school, on the other hand, engages the developing person in an organized quest for understanding. It says: apply your mind to a series of studies in order to gain a critical perspective on your environment.

The foregoing is true as far as it goes, but it does not go far enough. Homes and faith communities nurture, but they also educate, albeit less conspicuously. Schools educate, but they also nurture, albeit less prominently. Illustrations are not hard to find: a dinnertime discussion of an election campaign, or a talk between parent and child to help the latter analyze feelings of resentment towards a sibling, are close parallels to what might occur in a social studies class and in a health class at school. Similarly, an explanation from the pulpit of the meaning embedded in a scriptural passage and a discussion of the same in a Sunday school class correspond to ways in which a Shakespearean passage might be dealt with in the English period at school. Conversely, the affirming look or word used by a teacher to help students develop confidence; the insistence on orderly behavior and careful work; the showing of a film that depicts the miracle, as it were, (not just the concept) of nature's self-maintenance through the food chain – all those are nurturing activities, shaping attitudes rather than scrutinizing them in "educational" fashion.

A teacher, therefore, educates and nurtures; these processes are interwoven and inseparable. The same is true of the parent and of the clergy(wo)man, though the proportion of educating to nurturing may not be the same as with the teacher. We could say that all three are "educators and nurturers" or "fosterers or facilitators of human development." But those are unwieldy labels, which the economy of ordinary speech tends to reject. It is simpler and more natural, at least in the case of the teacher, to speak of an educator, understanding that the role encompasses both educating and nurturing.

You may be willing to accept the contention that a teacher educates *and* nurtures while not being prepared to grant that a teacher should do so in religious matters. Could not, should not, a teacher's educating and nurturing be restricted to the secular realm, leaving home and faith community to concern themselves with the religious realm? This question requires us to take up the next set of concepts – religion and secularity.

Religion and Secularity

Ian Kelsey's statement, cited in Chapter 1, succinctly expresses a prevailing conception of the difference between religion and secularity: "The school deals with a worldly or secular or non-religious sense of things. The church turns the world upside down and views things from a purely spiritual sense of things."[2] In this view there are worldly matters, the knowledge and control of our bodies and minds, of our material and social environment; and there are spiritual matters, separable from the former, pertaining to a power above the material order, to gods or God, to the transcendent, and so forth.

But does this dichotomy bear the test of reality? Let us first consider religion. Ninian Smart's six dimensions of a religion provide a useful checklist. A religion, he observes, normally entails: a system of doctrines; myths in the sense of stories that embody "the relation between the transcendent and the human and worldly realm;" ethical norms; rituals, such as worship or initiation ceremonies; inner feelings, both spontaneous and induced by rituals or another dimension of religion; and a visible social/institutional structure.[3]

It becomes apparent that each dimension of a religion incorporates secular elements. To give an example of each: the Christian doctrine of salvation through Christ encompasses divine action and a human response, namely, the conforming of one's "secular," everyday life to Christ's teaching and example. The Jewish myth of creation and fall, expressed in images drawn from earthly human experience, reveals the human condition as much as it does God's attributes. The ethics of Islam requires the Moslem to believe in "Allah, the last Day, the Angels, the Book and the Messengers," but also "to spend of your sustenance, out of love for Him, for your kin, orphans, the needy, the wayfarer, those who ask and for the emancipation of slaves . . . to fulfill the contracts which you have made; and to be firm and patient in suffering and adversity and throughout all periods of panic."[4] Ritual, too, is constituted of both other-worldly and earthly elements, as epitomized by a Hindu's way of starting the day:

> To prepare his mind and heart for prayer, breathing exercises are most important, as breath is life, the most real thing about the body. He breathes out and in, then for a moment stops breathing; he breathes first through one nostril, then the other, and with each breath repeats to himself the word "Om," the shortest form in which one can name the Infinite Spirit.[5]

The inner religious experience that may be engendered by such ritual blends spiritual and material reality, as occurs also on those occasions when we experience a natural phenomenon (e.g., a sunset) not just sensibly and esthetically but also numinously. A visible social structure, the sixth dimension of a religion, is perhaps by definition "secular;" the point to be noted here, however, is that the most "spiritual" activities of a religion require institutional forms, as the monastic system in Buddhism illustrates.

Religions, then, incorporate the secular, but is the converse also true? Does our secularity, our concern with daily living, necessarily entail religion? Let us consider an example.

In a public library near my home hangs a poster showing a young woman running. Ponytail flying, head erect, she is silhouetted against a sky which reaches an intensity of brightness at her feet, as though they move with the strength of the rising sun. The four words on the poster are,"I believe in me."

Jogging is a mundane activity, a form of physical exercise, a source, sometimes, of physical aches and pains. It is unspectacular, a part of many people's daily routine, like packing a lunch or washing the dishes. Yet, as the poster reveals, it can have meaning far beyond its physiological function. It can be an expression of fundamental beliefs about human worth, about the beauty and the challenge of life, about freedom. An eminently secular activity, therefore, can resonate with ideas and ideals perceived to be of ultimate worth. In that respect, the activity becomes religious.

Here we are speaking of religion rather than of *a* religion having the six dimensions described above. Religion in this general sense refers to human beings' need for meaning and value in their lives. It entails existential questions, such as: why am I here? what is my relationship to nature and to other people? why must we suffer? what is worth striving for, dying for? The religions of mankind can be thought of as diverse ways of responding to such questions.

It may be asserted that secular life, while it can have the religious overtones described, need not do so. Secularity is able to stand on its own feet, as it were. Life can be lived without ultimacy. But can it, and still be worth living?

A life without a religious perspective is what Wildred Cantwell Smith would describe as a life without faith.

> The opposite of faith in this sense is nihilism: a bleak inability to find either the world around one, or one's own life, significant; an absence of mutuality, in that one cannot respond either to the universe or to one's neighbor knowing that one will be responded to; an almost total dependence upon immediate events coupled with a sense that immediate events cannot really or for long be depended upon; a sense of lostness. The current terms for this are alienation, loss of identity, uncommittedness.[6]

Faith gives to human life its rich humanity.

> At its best [faith] has taken the form of serenity and courage and loyalty and service: a quiet confidence and joy which enable one to feel at home in the universe, and to find meaning in the world and in one's own life, a meaning that is profound and ultimate, and is stable no matter what may

happen to oneself at the level of immediate event. Men and women of this kind of faith face catastrophe and confusion, affluence and sorrow, unperturbed; face opportunity with conviction and drive; and face others with a cheerful charity.[7]

Such faith can be induced and expressed by a traditional religion – that has been and continues to be the case for many people of great faith – but it is not restricted to "religious" people. The "secularist" too can be a person whose spirit, not confined to the narrow bounds of a life dominated by here-and-now considerations, reaches out to ideals never yet attained but inviting ultimate allegiance.

We may be inclined to view the scientific mentality as either an exception to, or a refutation of, the necessity of faith. In a true sense, however, one can speak of the faith of scientists. Cantwell Smith explains:

> I mean their faith in science, in the spirit of science: in science not as an objective actuality in disparate parts, but as an elusive and integral dynamic of which the outward expressions at any given moment, although worthy, are always and in principle inadequate and to be superseded – a dynamic that is both demanding and rewarding, in which they delight to be involved, and in which their involvement gives meaning to their work and even in some degree to their life. This faith undergirds and informs and elicits and transcends their work. Their beliefs (the concrete parts of the specific sciences of the day) come and go; but their faith, with all its ultimate ineffability, persists. As long as it persists, the scientific tradition will creatively flourish; what would be the meaning and contour of a dying of that faith it is hard to say, although obviously it could die.[8]

In the abstract, then, it is possible to isolate religion and secularity. Religion may be defined as knowledge of, and responsiveness to, the transcendent reality which makes existence ultimately meaningful and valuable.[9] Secularity may be defined as knowledge and use of existents insofar as their immediate, functional purposes are concerned. In reality, however, religion and secularity are – or, for the sake of a truly human existence, should be – organically related to each other.

Educating Religiously and Educating Secularly

It has become customary in western society to think of religious education and secular education as separate entities, whether or not they occur under the same school roof. Bible study, catechesis,[10] Jewish religious study, or equivalent programs in other faith traditions are seen as wholly distinct from English, history, science, physical education, music and the like.

Such a separation, however, is inconsistent with the previously discussed relationship between religion and secularity. The impracticality of the separation also becomes apparent when one reflects on the various subjects of the curriculum. On the one hand, for example, Bible study necessarily examines secular features of human behavior, in biblical times and today. On the other hand, the humanities inevitably reveal mankind's striving towards, and tragic betrayals of, religious (i.e., transcendent, ultimate) ideals. Science leads to wonder in the face of the natural world's inexhaustible beauty and mysteriousness, and demands attention to issues of the human worth of various scientific discoveries – issues which cannot be addressed on the basis of the scientific data alone but require consideration also of the purpose of human existence. Mathematics, which on the surface seems far removed from religion, awakens reflection on the infinite, the abstract and the real, unity, multiplicity, nothingness. All of this may appear to be lightyears away from learning how to add and multiply in elementary school, yet that is the time to start seeing mathematics, not just as convenient skills or mental games, but also as a way of comprehending, partially and imperfectly, the magnitude and order of the universe. (The concept of "lightyears" exemplifies this function of mathematics, incidentally.)

If examination of the curriculum shows religious education and secular education to be inseparable, this impression is confirmed if we recall the unity of nurturing and educating, discussed earlied. The mathematics teacher who (hypothetically) is only concerned with transmitting to students one or more of the logical systems comprised by mathematics, fails in nurturing. Such a teacher neglects to sustain and enhance the students' sense of worth as human beings, and to project to them – by word, enthusiasm, silent wonder – the conviction that mathematics provides an entry into realms of meaning that transcend mathematics. The nurturing teacher, on the other hand, heightens the students' self-perceptions as persons of transcendent dignity invited to partake of a transcendent universe. The nurturing teacher, in other words, is engaged in religious education.

At this point you, as a teacher or someone empathizing with teachers, may protest: "Too much!" Already heavily burdened, can teachers of the secular subjects really be expected to deal with the profound concepts and sensibilities encompassed in religious education?

A distinction must be made between teaching religion and educating religiously. The former term denotes the systematic treatment of religious concepts in formal courses, which require preparation and class time as do other courses and should accordingly be figured into the workload of the teachers concerned. "Educating religiously," however, refers to the activity of potentially all teachers, whether or not they teach religion courses as such. It is not esoteric activity. It means, quite simply, educating. It means fostering the development of beings who are constituted of both secular and religious capacities – human beings whose nature it is to seek mastery of specific mental and physical tasks *and* the integration of those tasks in an ultimately meaningful and worthwhile whole. Rather than being a burden, this dual focus for teaching and learning is natural. Teachers who are determined to deal only with the secular dimension of their subjects have a much harder – I would say impossible – task, because they must constantly be on guard against doing or saying anything which might affect, positively or negatively, students' awareness and appreciation of the transcendent and ultimate in human existence.

Educating religiously, then, is not confined to religion programs; it can be done in so-called secular fields – English (Chapter 3), history and other social studies, and, as suggested above, in mathematics and all the other subject areas in ways appropriate to them; it can be done through opening exercises (see especially Chapter 4); it can be done through extra-curricular activities, whether explicitly religious in character (e.g., the Inter-school Christian Fellowship program) or "secular" in character (e.g., a choral group's inclusion of religious hymns in its repertory, or an athletic team's taking seriously the values that transcend game skills and wins-losses records); it can be achieved through conversations in which the teacher evinces interest in, and provides affirmation of, students' religious perceptions and activities.

Educating religiously and educating secularly are pervasive, natural, interwoven aspects of the work of teachers. The fact, however, that (potentially) all teachers share in them does not obviate the necessity or at least the desirability of some division of labor. Every teacher is a teacher of English, but we still need English teachers. Similarly with religion.

Chapter 5 illustrates the possibility of a thirteen-year sequence of religious study, staffed in its upper stages by specialists. Such a program, geared to students' developmental levels, affords them opportunities to develop religiously, both through study of their own religious tradition (in this instance, Christianity) and through discovery of the insights and values characteristic of other traditions.

This reference to the diversity of religious traditions leads to the next set of concepts. Do not all religions support a common core of human values? Would it not be more practical and less controversial if multi-faith schools dealt only with those common values – if, in other words, they confined themselves to educating morally rather than religiously?

Educating Religiously and Educating Morally

In contrast to their long historical partnership, moral education and religious education are today separated by many philosophers and educators. Principles of morality can be formulated and put into practice without reference to religion, it is argued. If something is good, it is such not because an authority (a holy book, a church, God) says so, but because of its intrinsic and instrumental qualities, which are discernible by observation and reason. The purpose of moral education, according to this view, is to develop a person's capacity to make autonomous moral judgments (i.e., moral judgments not dependent on an external authority) according to the highest possible standards. Religious considerations can and should be left aside.

Contemporary moral education, it must be readily acknowledged, makes valuable contributions to human development. The Values Clarification approach, for example, leads students to identify values, to compare them with alternatives, to consider the consequences flowing from each, and in light of that reflection to make certain values their own. To cite another example, the cognitive-developmental approach associated with Lawrence Kohlberg fosters growth in moral reasoning ability through the enlargement of one's concept of justice. Such forms of moral education must not be belittled or blocked, but neither must they be construed as religionless, rational approaches which alone merit a place in schools.

All approaches to moral education are based in part on a conception, implicit or explicit, of the good. Values Clarification's conception might be described as the thinking, joyfully resolute person. Kohlberg's conception might be described as the just person who treats all other persons as his/her equals in human dignity. Conceptions of the good are ideals that beckon from beyond the theories and practices which constitute particular approaches to moral education. They can be contemplated and reflected on; they richly satisfy the mind; but they do not derive simply from observation and reasoning. They are part of the realm of transcendent value and meaning which may be termed religious. To say this is not to decry but simply to recognize the natural and proper state of moral education. The late Soviet educator, Vasily Sukhomlinsky, notwithstanding the "scientific, materialist world outlook" which Soviet schools are supposed to develop,[11] acknowledged this natural state when he wrote:

> From childhood a man should be encouraged to see the world in the light of an ideal so that his life should become a gradual ascent towards the ideal summit. An ideal is not a truth learnt by rote, which an individual can pronounce when called upon, but his heart-felt striving towards truth, justice and beauty.[12]

Educating morally, then, overlaps with educating religiously. Attempts to treat them as distinct and independent are bound to fail, though, superficially, the divorce may appear to have been effected. Allowing the two to work together will likely enhance the impact of each on students' development.

Given that there are values common to all religions and to "non-religious" approaches to morality, it makes sense to foster those values through the *combined* resources of religion and morality. Moreover, in addition to mutual reinforcement, this combination is likely to yield mutual enrichment, as is illustrated by what follows.

From the point of view of a student's moral development, encounters with world religions can engender new or renewed ethical insights. Here are some examples:

[An insight to be gained from Christianity]

Forgiveness is the life-blood of ethical action. If I forgive whole-heartedly, I regain the power to befriend, to serve, to criticize constructively and objectively (not pointlessly or vengefully). Likewise, if I genuinely accept forgiveness, I gain freedom from the shame or pride that inhibits me from taking similar ethical initiatives.

[An insight to be gained from Hinduism]

Each of us has a *dharma* to fulfill in life, that is, "no one exists without a purposeful place in the divine order of things." Thus I am neither ethically irrelevant (and hence cannot stand idle, saying, "What difference will my actions make anyway?"), nor an ethical factotum (and hence should not attempt to right all wrongs).

[An insight to be gained from Judaism]

Justice and mercy – these two ideals, though they are often blended indistinguishably in human acts and institutions, are each important as ethical guides. We must do justice, but not be limited by it; we must be people of mercy – forbearing and open-handed – but not be blinded by it to ongoing inequities.[13]

Similarly, from the point of view of the students' religious development, moral education emphasizing rationality can serve a valuable purpose. There is always a danger in religious development of becoming closed-minded, of mistaking a religious formulation for the absolute, which is ineffable. Thus, for example, the habit of thinking and saying "God's will be done," while laudable and indeed fundamental to most religious traditions, could override all considerations of personal ethical responsibility and rationality. One does not have to seek far for horrors that have been perpetrated or tolerated in the name of "God's will." Such travesties of divine intent would likely be less prevalent if people's religious development were accompanied by, and integrated with, moral development of the humane-rational type as exemplified in sound applications of Values Clarification and Kohlberg's theory.

In summary, there is everything to be gained if teachers undertake to educate religiously *and* morally. But is there not really a great risk in all this – the loss of the student's right to be free from indoctrination with ideas and values not of his choosing and not, however "common" they may be, universally embraced by mankind? This leads us to the final set of concepts to be considered: informing and influencing.

Informing and Influencing

A policy sometimes advocated by moral educators is that students be made aware of the diversity of human values, while being left entirely free in their value choices. There must be *teaching about,* rather than *teaching of,* morality. Similarly, if there is to be religious education, it should be *teaching about,* rather than a *teaching of,* religion.

The distinction does seem to have a basis in common experience. When we speak to an electrical appliance salesperson, or read the front page of the newspaper, or watch the television news, we may well want to be informed, not influenced. On reflection, however, it is apparent that "pure" information is the last thing we want. From the salesperson we wish to hear, not a list of the features of the various brands of appliance, but an honest and well-founded interpretation of their merits; from the front page of the newspaper we want to learn of local, national and international events which competent editors and writers judge to be most significant; and the same is the case with the television news. In each instance we think it proper to be guided to a degree by another person's judgment – in other words, to be influenced. Possible dissatisfaction with a salesperson or a newspaper or a television news show is based on not the *fact* but the *quality* of influence. We want well-informed and well-intentioned influence; in brief, informing and influencing go together.

As educating and nurturing are linked, so are informing and influencing – in the school as in society. A teacher worthy of the name is expected to influence students in wholesome directions while at the same time informing them. Students so influenced and informed are not deprived of their freedom of choice, but are given a better chance of exercising that freedom wisely.

An interesting illustration of the natural and proper combination of informing and influencing occurs in I.A. Snook's *Indoctrination and Education.* The author's conception of indoctrination centres on the idea of evidence.

> A person indoctrinates P (a proposition or set of propositions) if he teaches with the intention that the pupil or pupils believe P regardless of the evidence.[14]

> For the educator, the beliefs are always secondary to the evidence: he *wants* his students to end up with whatever beliefs the evidence demands. He *is concerned* with methods of assessing data, standards of accuracy, and validity of reasoning.[15]

In the second quotation I have italicized the words which reveal the influencing role of the teacher, who, from Snook's perspective, would do wrong to assume a purely informational role – i.e., remain indifferent as to whether students decide to value evidence or not.

I consider indoctrination to mean influence carried to excess. Indoctrinating, and other terms such as conditioning and brainwashing, refer to influencing unduly, whether by suppressing evidence, asserting one's authority in a coercive manner, or inveigling. It is worth noting that well-intentioned omissions can paradoxically have the effect of excessive influence. For example, if a health curriculum, to avoid risk of controversy, deals with human sexuality only in physiological terms, it may encourage students to regard sexual relations as primarily a physical matter rather than one involving such values as respect for persons, responsibility and commitment.

Common to all forms of undue influence by educators is an unjustifiable curtailment of the students' freedom to develop. It is ironic that religious education, and to a lesser extent, moral education, are sometimes deemed improper activities for a school because of their "indoctrinative" character, whereas the greater likelihood is that students are indoctrinated (i.e., unjustifiably restricted in their freedom to learn and develop) through the banning of religious and moral education.

Much hinges on the word "unjustifiably." When would it be justifiable to prevent, insofar as possible, any exposure of students to religious or moral information and influence (the two being linked, as already noted)? One circumstance, it has been argued, is the presence of children whose families hold beliefs and values which conflict with those of the majority.

It is certainly conceivable – and regrettably it has happened – that a child or children of a religious or ideological minority could be intimidated by words or activities deemed fitting and worthy for the majority. The conceivable, however, is not the necessary. The case material in the following chapters exemplifies how minorities can be shown respect in their divergence while majorities are allowed to develop religiously. The sensitivity of teachers, knowledgeable about the religious and moral values of the families they are serving, is the best safeguard against improper influence upon any individual student or group of students.

At the conclusion of this chapter, I may be accused of having attempted to influence the reader unduly. I have indeed tried to identify and endorse what appear to me to be natural, twinned processes of great importance to the all-round development of students. I *want* (recalling Snook's use of the term in the passage quoted above) teachers to engage in educating and nurturing, in educating religiously and educating secularly, in educating religiously and educating morally, in informing and influencing. But you, the reader, have the opportunity to concur or dissent, as you examine the cases in Chapters 3 to 7, which, from my perspective, disclose the possibility and the benefit of educating religiously in the multi-faith school.

Notes

[1]John Hull, "From Christian Nurture to Religious Education: The British Experience," *Religious Education,* Vol. 73, No. 2 (March-April, 1978), p. 124.

[2]Chapter 1, p. 4.

[3]R. Ninian Smart, "What is Religion?" *New Movements in Religions Education,* edited by Ninian Smart and Donald Horder, paperback (London: Temple Smith, 1978), pp. 14-16.

[4]The *Qur'an,* 2:117, cited by Jamal Badawi, "Islamic Ethics," *Ethics in Education,* Vol. 3, No. 6 (February, 1984) pp. 4-5.

[5]Florence Mary Fitch, *Their Search for God: Ways of Worship in the Orient* (New York: Lothrop, Lee and Shepard, 1947), p. 22.

[6]Wilfred Cantwell Smith, *Faith and Belief* (Princeton, New Jersey: Princeton University Press, 1979), p. 13.

[7]Ibid., p. 12.

[8]Ibid., p. 16.

[9]This definition fits both religions traditionally regarded as such and life stances such as secular humanism. However, it carries no implication that all religions and life stances are equally adequate and fulfilling forms of knowledge and response vis-à-vis transcendent reality.

[10]A term frequently used for religious education in the Roman Catholic tradition.

[11]"Fundamentals of Legislation of the USSR and the Union Republics on Education" (1973) cited by Zoya Malkova, *Education* (in the series: *The Soviet Union Today and Tomorrow* (Moscow: Novosti Press Agency Publishing House, 1981), p. 4.

[12]V. Sukhomlinsky, *V. Sukhomlinsky on Education,* introduced by Simon Soloveichik, translated by Katherine Judelson (Moscow: Progress Publishers, 1977), pp. 313-314.

[13]Donald Weeren, "Reflections on Five Religions," *Ethics in Education,* Vol. 3, No. 9 (May, 1984), p. 5.

[14]I.A. Snook, *Indoctrination and Education* (London and Boston: Routledge and Kegan Paul, 1972), p. 47.

[15]Ibid., pp. 55-56, (italics added).

3
Biblical Literature in the High School

by Mildred Burrows

Educators have often debated the feasibility of achieving both secular and religious objectives at the same time. My experience in teaching biblical literature at the high school level leads me to say that it is not only a feasible goal, but a readily achievable and rewarding undertaking. This chapter describes my experience under the following headings: History and Rationale; Structure and Content; Response and Value.

History and Rationale

A course in biblical literature at the Cobequid Educational Centre in Truro, Nova Scotia, came about more by chance than by design. For the school term of 1971-72, I developed an English course for grade ten honors students which was called World Literature, since it drew on many countries of the world for its material. Included in it was the epic literature from Genesis and several other Old Testament selections. This course received such an enthusiastic response from students and parents alike that we decided to introduce a half course in biblical literature at the grade twelve academic level.

When applying to the Nova Scotia Department of Education for permission to pilot this course, we presented the following rationale:

(a) The Bible (particularly the Old Testament) and Greek mythology are the two roots of English literature. Without a knowledge of both of these sources, any reader misses the symbols and allusions with which all great literature is permeated, and consequently fails to grasp the selection's in-depth meaning. Greek mythology is part of the English curriculum in Nova Scotia, so it is only fair that the Hebrew Bible be given an equal place.

(b) Most western literature expresses an intrinsic philosophy that stems from, or attempts to refute, the Judeo-Christian religion. It is difficult for students to understand the writer's slant, and even more so for a teacher to explain it to them, if they have no background knowledge of the Bible.

(c) It is the mark of an educated person to have a knowledge of the Bible. One needs that knowledge not only to fully appreciate literature, but also to fully understand our history and many current events, particularly those of the middle east. An appreciation of music and art is heightened by a knowledge of the Bible as well. One has only to visit a national art gallery anywhere in the western world to realize how strong is the biblical inspiration for the great masterpieces of all ages. How can one expect to appreciate the artist's interpretation, to say nothing of the theme, if one is unfamiliar with the character and/or event on which the painting is based?

We assured the Department of Education that the intent was to teach this course, as much as possible, from a literary point of view; however, we acknowledged the fact that as all great literature reflects the life and culture of the time and place in which it was written, it is impossible to study it without learning something of the history of the era. Likewise, because literature is a record of mankind's search for truth and knowledge, it is impossible to read it without learning something of the religious beliefs of the writers. We explained, however, that we would not become embroiled in fruitless arguments about the historicity of events recorded in the Bible, nor discuss the religious implications, but rather stress its literary qualities.

The Department gave its permission, and I began to teach a half course in biblical literature to grade twelve academic students in the fall of 1973. Over the years about twenty-five percent of the students have opted to take this course each term, although several other choices are offered at this level.

For several years I taught biblical literature as a half course. In 1980 we made some changes in the English curriculum at C.E.C. so that all half courses were eliminated. In order to keep biblical literature on the curriculum, we combined it with another half course to make up a full year's program, but this made it necessary for another teacher to take some of the classes in this course. This teacher, like myself, had taken a university course in biblical literature, and had enough background to feel comfortable in this program. I provided her with a folder of material, and we conferred as often as necessary to keep us moving along together, mainly so that the films, which were ordered in June to come at intervals throughout the next term, could be used by us both while they were at the school. I retired in June, 1983, so this past term (1983-84) two more teachers, men this time, have taken on sections of this course. They also have the background training that enables them to handle the content, and the teacher whom I helped has, in turn, worked closely with these two teachers.

The version of the Bible chosen for classroom use was the paraphrase, *The Way*,[1] and it was chosen for two reasons. For one thing, most conservative denominations which cling to the King James version do accept this paraphrase. The second reason is that, despite its poorer literary quality as compared to the Revised Standard or Jerusalem Bible, for example, it is very easily read. The students, particularly those brought up on the King James Bible, react very positively to its readability.

The Education Department does not provide Bibles for school use, so the teacher or school has to find some means of procuring a class set or, as is the case now, several class sets. This is a problem serious enough to preclude the introduction of this course in a school. However, the English department heads from two large schools in Nova Scotia came to me several years ago for outlines of my course; subsequently they started a similar one in their schools, so the problem can be surmounted, apparently. In our school the English department has a fund earned by sponsoring Neptune Theatre and other groups, and most of this money is spent on books that are not available from the School Book Bureau.

Structure and Content

The first year or two that this course was taught a chronological format was used; however, in two successive years our Association of Teachers of English included a workshop on the teaching of biblical literature at the annual conference. The first year it was led by Dr. James Perkin of Acadia University, and the second year by Dr. John Corston, who was then with the Atlantic School of Theology in Halifax. Both suggested the genre method, so I adopted that format although I have continued to fit it loosely within a chronological framework.

The literary genres found in the Bible are many. Those used include the following: epic, hero clusters, fable, poetry (which includes the taunt, riddle, incantation, oracle, victory ode, lament, hymns and love lyrics), laws, and the lecture or sermon, essay, proverb, history, biography, autobiography, epistle, short story, drama, and parable. Each genre is defined when it is introduced, whether this form is new to the student or serves merely as a review; however, the content is the more important reason for choosing a particular selection, so more time is given to that aspect.

Epic Literature

The course begins with the epic literature of Genesis, chapters one to eleven, with the most time being spent on the first three chapters. Background information is given so that the students will understand that the editors of Genesis drew on two traditions for the two creation stories to be found in these three chapters. The more "modern" account, which includes chapter one and the first three verses of chapter two, shows God as a powerful spirit whose commands bring action, whereas the more primitive story which follows depicts a God who manually creates and who talks with humans. The older account also presents a less orderly and logical pattern of creation. In addition, it has woman created to serve man, whereas chapter one states, "male and female created he them."

The symbols are listed and discussed to show what they mean when used by writers of subsequent literature. Titles of current films or novels which can be mentioned to show the influence of this selection on recent literature are, Fitzgerald's *This Side of Paradise,* Steinbeck's *East of Eden* or Constance Beresford-Howe's *The Book of Eve,* and also children's stories such as "Snow White," which use the apple symbol.

The curses are discussed, noting their similarity to Greek myths in that they provide an explanation for the natural phenomena of serpents crawling, pain with childbirth, human mortality and the necessity to work in order to survive.

For enrichment, modern versions of the creation story are included to show the continuing popularity of this early literature, and to note the variations in tone and style of the imitations. Included are the following:

(a) Recorded skits by Bill Cosby on Adam and Eve and the apple,

(b) Saint Sammy's version of creation in W.O. Mitchell's *Who Has Seen the Wind,*

(c) James Weldon Johnson's "Creation Story: A Negro Sermon,"

(d) The account in *Olde Charlie Farquharson's Testament,*

(e) Co Hodeman's animated film, "The Sandcastle."

It is interesting to note that these modern versions localize Eden to the writer's own homeland. Though two of these versions might be considered irreverent, I feel that students should be shown that biblical literature need not be stuffy and can be enjoyable.

A section of the Babylonian "Epic of Gilgamesh" is read to show that this and the creation story both allude to the time when humans realized that they had a spiritual as well as a physical nature and could assume some responsibility for their own actions and survival. Ralph Hodgson's "Eva" and F.R. Scott's "Eden" are read to compare these two interpretations of Eve's action. In "Eva," because Eve was seduced by the serpent, she symbolizes a sex object, but in "Eden" she is a strong leader who has the courage to challenge tradition and take the first step on the long road to truth and knowledge.

Works of art illustrating creation and the Garden of Eden are so readily available that it is easy to find several pictures for a display while the epic literature is being studied. Though far from great art, a comic strip from "B.C.," depicting a confrontation between the woman and the snake, could also be displayed.

One concept deriving from the first chapter of Genesis is that humans were put in charge of the earth to care for it. Two National Film Board films that comment on this are "One Man's Garden" and "Paradise Lost," and both are viewed at this time.

The story of Cain and Abel is read to explain the symbol of the mark of Cain and the concept of being one's brother's keeper. The story of Noah is included, noting the two versions given in the Genesis account, and the popularity of the ark image in cartoons is mentioned. The Tower of Babel story is read to show that Babel, when used in literature, symbolizes pride.

Hero Clusters

The "hero cluster" is a very common form of Old Testament literature. It compares closely to modern journalism in that it reports on some unusual event or outstanding feat that has taken place, and also in that several versions or perspectives of one exploit were sometimes told, or more likely, were altered somewhat as they were passed down through centuries until collected and edited by Old Testament scribes about 700 to 500 B.C. Naturally, these accounts vary considerably in detail, although the essential facts have usually come through intact, and it is interesting to note the several ways in which the Old Testament editors have incorporated the varying accounts into one coherent story. Some of these heroes make one brief cameo appearance, but the greater ones require several chapters or almost an entire book in order to record all of their exploits.

The heroes of these clusters, who lived from approximately 1800 to 900 B.C., are the patriarchs Abraham, Isaac and Jacob, the leaders Moses, Joshua, Samson and David, the prophets Samuel, Elijah and Elisha. Several women, too, made the hall of fame. The best known are Sarah, Hagar, Rachel, Miriam, Jael, Deborah, Delilah, Hannah, and David's wives, Michal, Abigail and Bathsheba.

In the case of the later heroes such as King David and Samuel, the clusters are complemented by actual biography, though these historical accounts are rarely as fascinating as the clusters are. One case in point is the story of David and Goliath. The historic account of Goliath's demise occupies one verse (II Samuel 21:19) whereas the story told in I Samuel, chapter seventeen, was so well polished by many tellings that it fits the definition of the modern short story, and is known by everyone. David does not enter into the historic account as he apparently was not credited with the giant's slaughter until he had become the famous leader of his people.

Selections to illustrate the hero cluster genre are chosen from the books of Genesis, Exodus, Joshua, Judges, and Samuel. Students are familiarized with the characters and exploits of figures to whom allusions are frequently made in much that has been written in the last twenty centuries. All who read literature should be able to recognize their names and appreciate their significance.

Christopher Fry's play, *The Firstborn,* is read during the teaching of the hero clusters since Moses is one of the important heroes. Newspaper clippings and magazine articles that refer to Abraham as the progenitor of both the people and the problems of the middle east should be displayed on the bulletin board at this time. Musicians, artists and writers have drawn so heavily on these heroes for their creative expression that one has no problem in finding material to enrich this section of the course, and it becomes merely a matter of the teacher's personal choice.

The Fable

The only biblical fable is found in Judges, chapter nine, and is told by Jotham in his hour of extremity. In this fable it is not Aesop's animals that talk and take on human characteristics, but a grove of trees.

Hebrew Poetry

Hebrew poetry is known by its parallel structure, but there is no difficulty in recognizing it in most modern translations, as it is set up in the form we use. Poetry is the oldest form of any culture's literature. Being more easily memorized, it is more readily passed down the generations in an intact form. Unrhymed in the original, Hebrew poetry translates into English with little loss of its poetic qualities.

In Hebrew literature, the oldest fragment of poetry is a boast by a man called Lamech and it is found in Genesis, chapter four. In it Lamech tells his wives that if Cain's death is to be avenged seven times, then Lamech has been avenged seventy-seven times by killing a youth who did him an injury. Obviously it is to this fragment that Jesus refers when answering Peter's question about how many times one is required to forgive an injury.

Other early poetic fragments are the taunts which apparently were employed merely to incite enough anger to get a battle started, but most students can recognize themselves, a few years back, in similar situations on elementary school playgrounds. Incantations, such as "The Song of the Well," are brief but probably developed over the centuries into the longer psalms and temple rituals. Samson's riddle is the only one recorded in the Bible, but apparently was as popular as a form then as it is today.

The oracles of Balaam make an interesting comparison to some of the Greek oracles composed by the priests at Delphi. Balaam's oracles are found in Numbers, beginning in chapter twenty-two. This story also explains why the name "Balaam" denotes an abuser of horses.

Two early poems are the victory odes composed and sung by Miriam and Deborah. Although these two women lived more than a century apart, their poems are similar in form and content. Both praise God for his greatness in overcoming the enemy in the face of great odds, they describe the situation through which God has safely taken them, and they express the usual philosophy of the victor in assuming that God hates their enemies as greatly as they do. Miriam's Ode is found in Exodus, chapter fifteen, and Deborah's Ode is in Judges, chapter five. These two poems make an interesting comparison if taken up in one class period.

Young people today are so inured to eroticism that the Songs of Solomon do not embarrass them even when read aloud as a dialogue with a chorus. They do appreciate the lovely imagery brought out through the use of similes, a necessary technique among primitive people whose language development is still at the concrete stage. Although the Bible is not noted for its humor, the students invariably laugh at one simile. In extolling the girl's attractiveness, the man lists her beauty points and ends by comparing the whiteness of her teeth to newly washed wool, and then adds the phrase ". . . perfectly matched with not one missing." Today's students laugh because young people do not appreciate the magic of modern dentistry. It is pointed out that this poem was included in the biblical canon because it was considered an allegory, with Solomon representing God and the girl God's chosen people.

Several psalms, sufficient for a class session, are chosen from several time periods to show varying philosophies. A few years ago, Psalm 137 was made into a popular song, "By the Rivers of Babylon," which many students recognize, so that psalm is a good choice, but the violence expressed in its final verse surprises the students. Although the psalms were once credited to King David, who probably did write several, including the twenty-third psalm, most were composed later as was the case with Psalm 137, obviously written at the time of the exile about 597 B.C.

The most elaborate acrostic, of the many examples in biblical poetry, is Psalm 119. The students read a part of it to see that the more complex the poetic form, the more difficult it is to make a coherent statement. This fact is apparent in this poem though the features of an acrostic are lost in the translation.

David's beautiful lament on the deaths of Saul and Jonathan is one that all students should know, and the other lamentations, found in the book of that name, tell of the fall of Jerusalem to the Babylonians. The poet's heavy dependence on personification is noted. Four of these poems were originally in an acrostic form.

Shortly before Christmas is a good time to read some of the poetry from Isaiah which forms the basis of several arias in Handel's *Messiah* and the Christmas spiritual, "Go Tell It on the Mountain." These selections are familiar to many students, although few of them have been aware of their biblical source.

Laws

Many laws are recorded in the books of Exodus, Leviticus and Deuteronomy. Like all laws, these were made to enable mankind to live in harmony with god(s) as well as with the other members of the tribe or clan. Religious laws govern ritual, and the actions and attitudes that please and placate one's god(s), while social laws deal with crime, health, civil problems, and family relationships.

The students read the Decalogue and note that the first three laws are purely religious, the fourth and fifth are both religious and social, while the last five are social. Of these, the sixth, seventh and eighth deal with actions, the ninth with words and the tenth with thoughts. The students also read a number of laws chosen from Leviticus or Deuteronomy that are representative of several types. These laws are discussed in an attempt to determine why many of them are still in force, while others no longer apply.

Essays and Lectures

Essays are found in Proverbs and Ecclesiastes, but those in the latter book are so cynical and pessimistic that I do not use them. Students enjoy the essay in Proverbs which warns a young man against the wiles of prostitutes. Also we read aloud from that book two or three of the chapters which record the wise nuggets of Hebrew folklore collected over the centuries. One day as we read through one of these chapters, a boy exclaimed aloud, "So that's where my grandmother gets all the clever advice that she keeps throwing my way." I fully expected a visit from the irate grandmother of a disillusioned grandson, but none ensued.

Lectures or sermons are to be found in any of the books of the prophets. Many of these are in poetic form, but others are written in prose. The students enjoy the short book of Joel for its vivid imagery and use of metaphor.

History, Biography and Autobiography

Although much of the Bible is historical, it contains only bits and pieces of textbook-type history, and this is found mainly in Kings, which tells of the reigns of the kings from the time of Solomon to the fall of Jerusalem. Parts of the two books of Samuel were obviously written as biography, but the editors interspersed it with hero clusters, so it is difficult to separate one from the other.

The Ezra/Nehemiah account of the rebuilding of the temple at Jerusalem after the return from exile is autobiographical, and, in the New Testament, part of Luke's account of the Acts of the Apostles is written in the first person.

Epistle

One usually thinks of an epistle as being a New Testament feature, but letters are also found in the book of Ezra. Students who have studied ancient history are surprised to discover that letters written by the kings Artaxerxes and Darius have been preserved for posterity in this book.

The Short Story

Although the short story form was not defined as a literary genre until the nineteenth century, there are, besides the tale of David and Goliath, several other stories in the Bible that fit the modern definition. Two of these, written in protest of the rabid nationalistic fervor that swept Israel after the return from exile, are the books of Ruth and Jonah. The romantic story of Ruth makes pleasant reading, but students fail to notice the subtle comment with which the story ends. Ruth was a Moabite, a nation despised by the Hebrews, but the last verse tells us that her great grandson was the famous King David. When Ruth was written, all foreign wives were facing expulsion in an attempt to keep the Hebrew nation pure. Few readers in that time would fail to spot the implication in the book's final verse.

The book of Jonah tells a fantastic tale of a very reluctant missionary. Here, the message is that God is not the exclusive property of the Hebrews, so foreigners need not be feared. On the other hand, the book of Esther is entirely secular and very nationalistic in tone. All three books are short and interesting and so can be readily assigned for outside reading. Because all three characters are so frequently mentioned in literature, the students should know their stories.

Drama

The closet drama of Job is too long and difficult for this course, but two sections are read. The prologue and epilogue, which can be summarized briefly by the teacher, are written in prose and based on a folktale current at the time of writing. The remainder of the book is in poetry, some of it magnificent. Students read the chapters which describe Job's code of ethics, for it gives a good insight into the lifestyle of a prosperous landowner of that era. God's answer to Job is also read, for here the poet reaches the acme of his art.

The Parable

Parables are found in the New Testament, and almost every student is familiar with the Good Samaritan and the Prodigal Son, so those two and several others are read and discussed.

Examples of Assignments

Many of the assignments given in this course are in the form of creative writing. Some examples follow:

(a) Choose an incident involving a biblical hero and rewrite it in the form of a dialogue.

(b) Write a modern psalm.

(c) Write a short story or play based on the rivalry which existed between Sarah and Hagar.

(d) Write a victory ode about a modern event, but following the style of Miriam and Deborah.

(e) Write a story or poem, set in modern times, but dealing with the brotherly conflicts experienced by Joseph and his brothers or by Cain and Abel.

Other assignments were similar to the following:

(a) Explain why the creation stories, though composed thousands of years ago, are still universally known.
(b) One comment in Genesis states, "And in thee (Abraham) shall all families of the earth be blessed." Discuss the contribution which Abraham's descendants have made over the centuries to western civilization in order to prove or dispute the statement.
(c) Discuss the several methods that the editors of the Old Testament used in order to incorporate several versions of an event into one coherent story.
(d) Account for the differing points of view expressed by (1) the writer of the book of Exodus, (2) Christopher Fry in *The Firstborn,* and (3) Marjorie Pickthall in "A Mother in Egypt."

A good test question is to give several quotations, each of which includes a biblical symbol or allusion, and have the students find the symbol and explain its significance to the quotation.

Response and Value

There have never been any problems with or complaints about this course in the school, so if students or parents have been disgruntled, they have kept it to themselves. We have refused to get involved in any arguments about the content of the course; if a question that might have led to a controversy came up, it was referred back to the student's parents or religious leader to answer.

An important requisite for teaching this course, probably more important than one's training in biblical literature, is the teacher's attitude towards students. Because there is so much in the content that could be controversial, it is essential that the teacher consistently treat the students with courtesy, and respect all of the wide diversity of religious beliefs that can be found in any class. Over the years I have had in my classes some non-Christian students as well as members of all of the conservative and liberal Christian denominations to be found in Nova Scotia. Any teacher who resorted to sarcasm, which builds up resentment and animosity, would soon discover that the students could readily find a wealth of ammunition in this course with which to "get" the teacher.

The avoidance of ill-feeling and controversy may be seen as a mark of the course's success, but what has been its impact in positive terms? My students acquire a basic understanding of how the Bible was written and edited, and many find pleasure in reading it. I recall one parents' night when a mother's remark, "We could never get our children interested in reading the Bible, but now I often see Allan reading his, and he seems to enjoy it," was followed later that evening by a father's comment, "When I came home last night, Danny was entertaining his brothers and sisters with a dramatic reading of the description of the leviathan found in the book of Job."

Such favorable verdicts should not be taken to mean that the course is appreciated by all students. Their reactions range from comments such as, "I didn't like the course as I don't believe in the Bible, so I consider that reading it is a waste of time," and "I didn't really learn much as I have been going to Sunday School ever since I was small," to "I had no idea that the Bible was such a wonderful book," or "My parents take a literal view of the Bible, and I could never see much sense in it, but now I think it is a most fascinating book." Some students admitted that they had never opened a Bible before they came to my classes. Most of these found what they encountered within its covers to be most interesting. Generally, students in this course react the same as in any course, for some find it boring and learn little, while others are enthusiastic and learn a great deal. Students who have gone on to university often make a point of dropping in to tell me that they did not fully appreciate the course until they began to study the humanities at college.

With its emphasis on the literary aspect of the Bible, this course may well take away some of the mystique and sacredness with which the Bible is generally associated; however, it may also take away the erroneous idea that the Bible is a sacred symbol whose sole use is its presence in the home. The old joke about the family Bible being left lying so long on the parlor table that it eventually settled into the varnish is based on fact. The Bible may still be a bestseller, but it is seldom read by those who buy it.

It is not just the language of the traditional (King James) version that has made the Bible difficult to read, for its format makes no attempt at a logical chronology or a consistent literary style. This is very confusing to anyone who has had no explanation of when, how and why the various selections of the Bible were written. Consequently, those who determine to read it from cover to cover usually give up after the first encounter with a chapter of "begats."

While the course was proposed for, and can stand on, its literary merits, it does have religious implications. One may well ask why it is desirable that students be taught to read the Bible without compulsion and with enjoyment, and what will be gained by such a move, as far as their religious education is concerned.

It has been my experience that most students who take this course claim to belong to some Christian denomination, but only a very small percentage have any knowledge of the Bible, or even a familiarity with the so-called children's Bible stories. The majority of the adults in all denominations of the church today have little knowledge of the Bible, particularly the Old Testament. This same Bible, however, traces Christianity from its beginning back through its roots in another world religion, but unless one reads and becomes familiar with this, how is one to understand where we are now in relation to our beginnings? The Bible follows the progressive growth of faith in Abraham's one God from the primitive concepts of what that God demanded of his followers, up through the centuries to Christ's vision of a heavenly father who loves the sinner and welcomes home the fallen. The Bible has had a tremendous impact on every aspect of our western civilization – not just our theology, but our philosophy, our morals, our social mores, and our sense of social justice as well as our cultural life. People who have little knowledge of the Bible fail to understand the thinking behind the issues over which the church and society are agonizing today, issues such as capital punishment, our responsibilities to third world people, or the ordination of women or of avowed homosexuals to the priesthood or ministry. Unaware of the progression of revelation that is obvious to most people who know the Bible, many of those who do not read it are inclined to think that whatever was acceptable and right in Grandfather's time must still apply.

In today's complex and troubled world there is great need for young people to be brought in touch with their religious roots, in order that they may establish some direction in life, a direction that can be found in the Bible. One day a student paused on his way out of class to remark, "I read the book of Mark last night. Isn't it sad that in Christ's teaching is the formula that would eliminate all of this world's problems, and we have, for twenty centuries, refused to listen to him." Personally, I feel that much of the aimless searching for identity today by many people, adults as well as young people, is caused by their lack of knowledge of our heritage. Those familiar with the Bible, whether affiliated with any particular religion or not, have access to an understanding of the meaning of life and death, and of their place in this world and of their responsibility to others. Such fortunate ones do not need to turn, as so many do, to drugs or alcohol, to religious cults or to suicide in an attempt to find an answer to their questions or to cope with their anxieties. Although the biblical literature course is not designed to teach religious truths, it can provide students with the key that will enable them to find them for themselves.

Many teachers doubtless hesitate to introduce a course of this type because of the fear of arousing controversy; however, the record of my teaching the course for ten years without incident, and of three other teachers following my footsteps without difficulty, proves that it can be done. Its educational benefits are not limited to a greater appreciation of literature, though that is a sufficient recommendation, but extend to greater religious understanding. The fact that the denominational backgrounds of teachers and students may differ is unimportant in the face of the basic values and ideas encountered in a study of biblical literature.

Notes

[1]Editors of "Campus Life Magazine," *The Way* (Wheaton, Illinois: Lyndale House Publishers, 1972).

4
Daily Readings/Prayers:
The Toronto Model

Our case studies are concerned with religious development in schools with religiously heterogeneous student populations. Religious development refers to growth in knowledge of, and responsiveness to, that which is of deepest meaning and value in human existence. The home and the church, synagogue, mosque or other faith community are expected to make contributions to religious development. Is the multi-faith school also able to make a contribution? That is the question which the case studies address. It is hoped that they will assist educators in forming their own approaches to the school's role in religious development.

In this chapter we examine the practice of daily readings/prayers in Toronto public schools. The purpose is not to survey all or a representative sample of Toronto's one hundred-plus elementary schools and thirty-plus secondary schools; the purpose is to disclose the possibilities of the Toronto program. The case study is divided into five sections: the genesis and nature of the Toronto program; practices in an elementary school; practices in another elementary school; practices in a high school; conclusions.

Genesis and Nature of the Toronto Program

In the late 1970s the Toronto School Board confronted the problem of honoring Ontario regulations on opening exercises while respecting the religious diversity of the Toronto school population. The regulations call for the opening or closing of each school day "with religious exercises consisting of readings of the Scripture or other suitable readings and the repeating of the Lord's Prayer or other suitable prayers."[1] The Board, judging that the exclusive use of the traditional format – a Bible reading followed by the Lord's Prayer – did not suit contemporary circumstances, established a committee to develop alternatives.

Assistant Superintendent Ouida Wright formed a committee of some thirty-five people by inviting all of Toronto's known religious bodies, as well as a number of other potentially interested agencies, such as the teachers' federations, to send representatives. Even the groups which declined the invitation expressed support for the undertaking and the wish to be informed of the outcome.

The committee decided to develop a collection of readings and prayers from a variety of traditions "to provide focus for the silent meditation of the students, and to increase student and staff awareness of the many religious and cultural traditions of the students in the city's schools" (p.i). Dr. Donald Beggs, a Toronto school administrator who served on the committee and performed much of the editorial work, commented on the purpose of the collection. The committee, he said, believed the individual student would find opening exercises more meaningful and comfortable if content drawn from his/her own faith tradition were included. The undertaking, he added, exemplifies the public school's sensitivity to every student and the value it attaches to the religious and cultural variety of the school population.

The committee sub-divided into smaller units, each representing a single faith and charged with gathering material in consultation with its particular religious constituency. According to Rev. George McClintock (a member of the committee who also assisted in editing and revising the collection), material proposed for inclusion was to meet these criteria: acceptable to the faith group; not repugnant to any other faith group; free from invidious comparisons; as far as possible, suitable for reading without comment, and understandable by the majority of the students. Submissions by the sub-units were considered by the full committee, which was the final arbiter of what would appear in the collection.

The lengthy meetings required to accomplish the committee's task were accepted ungrudgingly by the members. From Dr. Begg's comments one gathers that discussions were frank and friendly, and that there was a shared sense of commitment and achievement in a worthwhile undertaking.

One potential source of division among the committee was the tenor of certain readings recommended on behalf of secular humanism. The presence of readings in the secular humanist tradition, it should be noted, is consistent with the concept of religion as "intimate and ultimate concern – convictions and activities dealing with the ultimate meaning of existence" (p. 212). The contentious selections contained statements that explicitly questioned the validity of theistic faiths. The committee, albeit with reluctance on the part of some members, was able to reach a compromise: some passages were deleted, others, such as the following, were retained.

> There is no need to assume
> The existence of a God
> Behind the community
> Of persons[;] the community
> Is the absolute
> (p. 215)

According to Dr. Beggs, the principle of the right to believe weighed with the committee. He suggested also that the explicit acknowledgment of an atheistic or agnostic position was preferable, considering the feelings of the children of humanistic persuasions, to the traditional exclusive use of the theistic Lord's Prayer in opening exercises in Ontario. It is worth noting, too, that each school is free to decide what pieces to use from the collection.

The first edition of the anthology was revised, enlarged and reissued in 1982. The table of contents of the 1982 version is reproduced here.

Table of Contents

The Introduction, after sketching the background and purpose of the collection, specifies the format for "opening or closing exercises in all Toronto schools:" ([p. ii])

  (a) O Canada

  (b) the reading of a minimum of one selection from the *Readings and Prayers;*

  (c) suitable comment by the teachers or principal, *if necessary,* concerning the origins of the selections used, *as indicated;*

  (d) silent meditation.

    The section on each faith begins with an overview of the faith, and typically describes its major festivals. This material is intended as a basis on which to make the possible comment, referred to in (c) above. A comprehensive calendar of religious and secular festivals is incorporated in the document, under the heading, "Special Days throughout the School Year," and is reissued annually to accommodate movable holidays. The calendar, too, aids in the selection of readings/prayers for a given day.

As the table of contents suggests, the number of selections from each faith varies. This reflects not any conscious apportioning of space, but simply the volume of selections submitted to the committee by its faith-subgroups. The length of the selections is also quite varied.

A tentative classification of the selections may help the reader visualize the make-up of the anthology. The examples serve to illustrate each category, but are not claimed to typify the collection.

Category I. A prayer addressed to a deity

Example:

> Thou art Mother,
> thou art Father,
> thou art Brother,
> and thou art Friend,
> thou art Knowledge,
> and thou art Wealth,
> Lord, my Lord,
> thou art all in all.

(Hinduism, p. 146)

Example:

> Remember us for life,
> King, who delight in life,
> And inscribe us
> In the Book of Life
> For your sake,
> God of life.

(Judaism, p. 176)

Example:

> O Lord, I am worried. I know that it does me no good to worry, but I cannot shake it off.
> It not only does no good to worry; it does harm. What I cannot change, I cannot change. But, meanwhile, if I am this caught up in worry, I'm apt to do poorly what I could do well.
> Help me to trust to you those concerns beyond my reach so that I may give my full attention to living each moment as it comes.

(Christianity, p. 129)

Category II.

A message addressed to humanity concerning a deity or a deity's expectations of humanity.

Example:

> Then Peter came to Jesus and asked, "Lord, if my brother keeps on sinning against me, how many times do I have to forgive Him? Seven times?"
> "No, not seven times," answered Jesus, "but seventy times seven."

(Christianity, p. 101)

Example:

> And worship God alone. Do not worship anything else with Him. And be kind to parents, to the relatives, to the neighbor who is near and the neighbor who is far, to those who happen to be with us, to those who travel on the way, and to those under your hands. God indeed does not love those who despise others and are proud of themselves.

(Islam, p. 160)

Example:

> With the coming of spring,
> There is blossom on every spray;
> In the same fashion,
> With the coming of inner devotion to God,
> All sentient creatures have an inner blossoming,
> And in this way the mind becometh fresh and green.
> Day and night repeating the Name of the Lord,
> Those who have seen God wash away all self-will.

(Sikhism, p. 234)

Category III.

A message addressed to humanity concerning humanity, without explicit reference to a deity.

Example:

> May my *enemies* be well, happy, peaceful and prosperous.
> May no harm come to them, may no difficulty come to them
> and no problem come to them, may they always meet with success.
> May they also have patience, courage, understanding and determination to meet and overcome inevitable difficulties, problems and failures in life.

(Buddhism, p. 33)

Example:

> If I let myself believe anything on insufficient evidence, there may be no great harm done by the mere belief; it may be true after all, or I may never have occasion to exhibit it in outward acts. But I cannot help doing this great wrong towards Man, that I make myself credulous. The danger to society is not merely that it should believe wrong things, though that is great enough, but that it should become credulous.

(Secular Humanism, p. 216)

Example:

> Tzu Yu asked about filial piety. Confucius said: "Nowadays a filial son is just a man who keeps his parents in food. But even dogs or horses are given food. If there is no feeling of reverence, wherein lies the difference?"

(Confucianism, p. 138)

A tentative allocation of the selections to the categories reveals the following distribution:

Categories

	I	II	III
Bahai	6		
Buddhism			7
Confucianism			4
Christianity	37	83	7
Hinduism	12	15	7
Islam	3	21	5
Judaism	15	18	2
North American Indian	3	2	
Other readings	18	6	21
Secular humanism		2	33
Sikhism	12	15	3
Zoroastrianism	1	1	1
	107	163	90

How has this multi-faith anthology been received? Reactions of teachers and administrators in the Toronto system appear to be favorable. A sampling of staff, conducted by school principals in preparation for the revision of the pilot edition, yielded requests for more material and for changes in its editorial organization, but no criticisms of the book's objectives or content. Educational jurisdictions elsewhere in Ontario and in other provinces have shown considerable interest, one board placing an order for 1500 copies. The following sketches of the anthology in use in three schools reveal its promise, as yet only partially realized.

Practices in Elementary School A

School A enrolls 450 students in kindergarten through grade 6. More than half the enrollment is in French immersion, that is, in classes in which Anglophone students are taught in French. Details of the school's religious composition were not available, but a multi-faith population can be inferred from requests for authorized absence from school on Jewish High Holy Days, and from declarations by Roman Catholics applying their school taxes to public, rather than Roman Catholic separate, schools. (The principal estimated that fifteen to twenty percent of the children are Roman Catholic.)

Selections for opening exercises are taken by rotation from the Toronto collection. Thus, a Bahai reading might be used on Monday, followed by a Buddhist reading on Tuesday, a Christian reading on Wednesday, and so forth. The rotation is not a matter of strict observance, and in any event it is interrupted by holidays or other special events. As examples the principal cited use of the series of Bible readings leading up to the nativity of Jesus, and the use of readings from the Confucian tradition on the occasion of a visit to the school by a group of scholars from China. The reader generally explains briefly whatever special occasion is being observed, unless the significance of the day is already very familiar.

The opening exercises are conducted over the public address system, generally by the principal or vice-principal. It is also common, however, for students to do the reading, the selection from the anthology sometimes being made by the students or by their teacher. The principal estimated that during that school year, students had been the readers about one-third of the time. Some had used French readings (the Christian and Jewish sections of the anthology contain French as well as English versions of many of the selections).

Opening exercises at School A were observed in a grade 5 class comprising twenty-eight children. Following announcements, the principal stated that this was Shrove Tuesday and that the beginning of Jesus' ministry was being commemorated. He then read the passage from Saint Luke's gospel (4: 16-20) relating how Jesus cited the prophet Isaiah in the synagogue of Nazareth:

> The Spirit of the Lord is upon me, because he has chosen me to bring good news to the poor. He has sent me to proclaim liberty to the captives and recovery of sight to the blind, to set free the oppressed and announce that the time has come when the Lord will save his people. (p. 64)

Following the reading, the principal said, "Please rise for a moment of silent prayer." After an interval, "O Canada," sung by children in French, was played.

Most of the children sat silently during the reading, but a few were conversing unobtrusively. It appeared that the reading had not registered strongly even with the silent ones, because when the class was asked an hour or so later, no student was able to recall what the reading had been about. Asked for any recollections of past readings, a number of students volunteered brief thoughts that had stayed with them:

"Always be happy"
"All human beings are alike"
"I am not perfect"
"About man and God"
"The happiness recipe" (Two heaping cups of patience, etc.)
"I love you"
"Angels coming down"
"Have sympathy for them who have done wrong."

All the recollections were of readings that had been done by students, and in three instances by the student volunteering the recollection. Nevertheless, the class did not favor the idea that the readings be done by students exclusively.

The students were asked to respond on paper to some of my questions. Favorable reactions to opening exercises prevailed over negative views, but most students appeared not to have conscious attitudes in either direction. Here are two of the most positive and two of the most negative views expressed (spelling errors having been corrected):

> I think that prayers are useful for people in another religion because they can learn about other religions.

> I think about what the true meaning of the prayer is. I listen very carefully to every word that is spoken. I think it's good that children have a chance to listen to a part of the Bible every morning. I do like listening to the morning prayer.

> [During the reading] I'm usually half asleep because most of the time I don't understand them.

> I think the Lord's Prayer is a waste of time.

Faced with the hypothetical situation of the school board's having to decide whether to continue the opening exercises, fourteen students voted in favor of continuance, seven voted against, and six registered ambivalent votes.

Practices in Elementary School B

School B enrolls about 170 students in kindergarten through grade 6. Located in a Portuguese neighborhood, the school draws some eighty percent of its enrollment from Roman Catholic Portuguese families, which typically have their children attend Sunday school classes and make their First Communion. The remaining twenty percent belong to Ontario-born, Protestant families. The school population as a whole, therefore, is Christian in background. Children of non-Christian faiths constitute only a tiny percentage of the enrollment.

Given the religious composition of the student body, readings/prayers chosen for opening exercises at the school are very often taken from Christian sources. Other religious traditions, however, receive some attention, especially in classes taught by Jewish or Moslem teachers. The variability is possible because at School B each teacher is responsible for conducting opening exercises in his/her classroom. A departure from this pattern occurs approximately every two weeks when the entire school gathers for a short assembly. Each class takes its turn in planning and conducting the assembly, which could consist of a prayer, a reading (whether individual or choral) and perhaps a dramatization. The assembly may take its theme from a festival occurring at the particular time of the year. According to the principal, students appear to like the assemblies, and the teachers, though initially a bit apprehensive about bearing the responsibility with their classes for conducting them, have shown their support of the practice.

Opening exercises were observed here in a grade 1 class. Some twenty-eight children, having removed boots and hung up their coats, were seated on a large mat, facing their teacher. Interspersed with some dialogue between teacher and class about recent activities or events, the opening exercises comprised the singing of "O Canada" by the children, and the singing of the "morning song" with the aid of a tape recorder. The morning song consisted of morning greetings and the following prayer:

Father, we thank Thee for the night
And for the pleasant morning light,
For the rest and food and loving care
And all that makes the day so fair.

Help us to do the things we should,
To be to others kind and good.
In all we do, in work and play,
To grow more loving every day.

As the same opening is used every day, the students knew the words, and sang them clearly.

When the writer asked the class whether they liked the opening activity, there was a loud chorus of approval. Why did they like it? The handful of answers suggest that the activity appealed in different ways to different children.

"You pray to God."
"I like singing O Canada." (2 responses)
"I like prayers." (2 responses)
"You ask God to help you."
"I like singing the morning song."

Asked whether they could suggest a different prayer to say at school, they seemed fully content with the prayer in use. (The prayer, in this instance, is not found in the Toronto anthology, although it corresponds closely to some passages appearing there.)

Practices in a High School

The high school I visited enrolls some 1350 students in grades 9 through 13. They are a culturally diverse group, including some 500 students of Chinese origin and a large contingent of Portuguese Catholics.

The material for opening exercises is taken from the Toronto anthology, supplemented by a variety of readings, ranging from a "Dear Abby" column to poems recommended by teachers. Selections are geared to the occasion, whether it be a death that touches the students (e.g., a fellow student, a John Lennon), an event in a place of conflict (e.g., Lebanon), or a day of special religious significance (e.g., Ash Wednesday). The teacher responsible for opening exercises said she would like to have Chinese used in the exercises from time to time, but Chinese-speaking students are reluctant due to sensitivity regarding differences in dialect among them.

Students enrolled in this teacher's Theatre Arts course take turns as readers, each student being expected to sign up for at least one day in the school year. When, as sometimes happens, a student demurs on the grounds of not being "religious," she points out that reading a passage from the anthology effectively does not require the conviction of faith, and also offers the student the option of proposing a reading from another source. Such proposals are almost invariably found appropriate by the teacher.

Opening exercises were observed in a geography class enrolling English-as-a-second-language students from the Orient. When the bell rang, the students rose and stood respectfully during the playing of "O Canada" over the public address system. Then a female student's voice, lacking in forcefulness and timing but not in sincerity, was heard reciting this prayer:

> For the one in need
> of your great love,
> we pray today.
> Lord, hear our prayer,
> hear our prayer.
>
> For our own lives,
> Lord, and the ones
> we touch from
> day to day.
> Lord, hear our prayer,
> hear our prayer.
>
> For the leaders of our nation, Lord,
> we pray for grace.
> Lord, hear our prayer,
> hear our prayer.
>
> For those in need,
> All need all around the world,
> give help, O Lord.
> Lord, hear our prayer,
> hear our prayer.

(p. 125)

As soon as the prayer was over, the business of the class began. The policy, however, is to have fifteen seconds for silent reflection following the prayer, whereupon the reader announces the number of the day in the five-day cycle. Another possible departure from the norm was technical in nature. The sound, somewhat muffled, seemed to come from the corridor rather than from a speaker in the classroom. Presumably a properly functioning classroom speaker would have made the opening reading easier to understand.

What do opening exercises mean to the students? The respecful silence noted by the writer in the geography class suggests a positive impact. The Theatre Arts teacher reported that once in a while colleagues and students come to her asking for a copy of what they have heard in an opening exercise. If opening exercises are omitted on a given day, because of a breakdown in the public address system, for example, students remark on their absence to her.

Two classes (a writing class for students, mainly from the Orient, acquiring the use of English, and a grade 12 social studies class) were asked to respond to the following question:

Think about what happens and what you feel and think about during the opening exercises (the playing of "O Canada" and the special reading) and write a paragraph or two telling your impressions.

Here are some of the responses:

Writing class

Readings and Prayers

1. "The reading sometimes has a loud echo for me. Even though I don't understand them all, but I surely understand those words all have the tendency to give us ideas about what is goodness and how to be good, and sometimes a warm blessing."

"O Canada"

2. "It reminds everybody that you are a Canadian. You are coming to school today and soon will have to make Canada a better country."

3. "I don't feel anything except the singing and reading. I don't want to bother what it is about, maybe I am too tired or too lazy to notice what is going on. Sometimes the school has another style of singing [O Canada], then I will try to listen to it."

Social Studies class

4. "I bow my head and think what I'm going to do that day or the night. I'm not very religious. I listen to the prayer and think of what it [is] saying. I try to relate the topic with what's going on but after it's finished it just vanishes."

5. "I think [of] what's going on in Canada, what I've heard or what I would like to happen in my country."

6. "It is good because it takes most if not [all] religions and thoughts in account. That's democratic and fair. Some are very lovely worded. However it gets tedious at times, but I suppose all things do."

7. "I feel somewhat if not totally apathetic towards the playing of the National Anthem. Along with the apathy there is a mixture of annoyance and resentment ... I do not have the choice on whether I want to stand or not ... I simply dislike being told to 'act out' something that particular moment."

To obtain an overall measure of the students' reactions, the scripts I received (twelve from the writing class, eight from the social studies class) were rated according to the following scale. The numbers in parentheses, referring to the excerpts quoted above, illustrate how the scale was applied.

++	Positive	(1) (2) (5) (6)
+	Less strongly positive	(4)
0	Not determinable from response	
−	Negative (i.e., student chooses not to listen)	(3)
--	Strongly negative (i.e., student dislikes or resents)	(7)

The summed ratings of all the scripts appear as follows:

Meaningfulness/affect as Perceived by Student

Readings and Prayers	Writing Class	Social Studies Class
++	6 (50%)	2 (25%)
+	Nil	5 (63%)
0	5 (42%)	1 (13%)
−	1 (8%)	Nil
--	Nil	Nil

"O Canada"		
++	9 (75%)	1 (13%)
+	Nil	3 (38%)
0	1 (8%)	Nil
−	1 (8%)	1 (13%)
--	(8%)	3 (38%)

While the two classes represent a substantial difference in cultural background, both responded positively to the reading and prayers, if we make allowance for difficulties the oriental students apparently had with comprehending the readings and prayers and articulating their reaction to them. In the case of "O Canada," there was a greater divergence of attitude between the two classes, raising a question about the assumption sometimes made that patriotic content in opening exercises is unifying whereas religious content is divisive.

Oral questioning of the social studies class usefully supplemented the written submissions. The attitudes of twelve students towards the readings and prayers are noted here:

Student 1. Readings have intellect, meaning, variety. "You pick up something."

Student 2. Usually ends up thinking about the reading. Sometimes caught short of time for thinking about it sufficiently.

Student 3. Looks forward to the reading. Has a moral. Nice poetry, interesting.

Student 4. Readings don't just look into religion, but poetry, thoughts; everyone (i.e., all traditions) has a chance.

Student 5. Listens to prayer usually if in the mood; tries to relate it to what's happening.

Student 6. Enjoys prayer because it has a message.

Student 7. Prays to God in her head, for family, friends, for the sick and dying as priest says we should. Gives her a chance to think.

Student 8. Thinks only some readings are good.

Student 9. Worries about what is to follow that day (e.g., a test); readings make you think a lot.

Student 10. Some of the readings are interesting.

Student 11. Thoughts of tests etc. tend to interfere with her attention to the readings and prayers.

Student 12. Reading many times has meaning for her. Strangely it coincides with what she has been thinking about.

Rating these oral responses according to the same scale used for the written responses, the writer arrives at this distribution:

++	7
+	4
0	1
–	0
--	0

Conclusion

This case study has attempted to shed light on the question of whether the multi-faith school can contribute to the religious development of its students. It examines one of several possible ways of fostering religious development, i.e., daily, public readings/prayers intended to prompt personal meditation.

Religious development is understood to mean growth in knowledge of, and responsiveness to, that which is of deepest meaning and value in human existence. The Toronto program clearly shows that it is possible for a multi-faith community to cooperatively assemble, and sanction for school use, materials expressive of humankind's most fundamental beliefs and values. The great diversity of traditions, each with its distinctive way of seeing and responding to reality, need not bar such an undertaking. Nor is it necessary that the various groups suppress what is most valuable in their eyes for the sake of consensus. It is necessary only to curtail explicit rejections of what another group or groups hold sacred. Thus, for example,

Readings and Prayers for Use in Toronto Schools includes both words from theistic traditions, fervently addressed to God as source of existence and value, and words that express faith in humanity alone. It is only frontal repudiation of each other's beliefs that undermines consensus.

The contrasting visions in the anthology, however, are accompanied by many statements diverse in origin but effectively one in substance. Thus, the Buddhist prayer cited earlier, "May my *enemies* be well, happy, peaceful and prosperous . . .," resonates in the words of Jesus, also cited, about forgiving "seventy times seven."

The *prima facie* significance of the Toronto readings and prayers in students' religious development needs to be verified. Evidence indicates that they do strike a responsive chord among students, but not as frequently or as strongly as they might if more attention were given to their effect. One principal reported that, notwithstanding his teachers' initial expression of enthusiasm for the multi-faith character of the collection, there had been no formal staff discussion of opening exercises for a year or so. Regular monitoring and attempts to improve meaningfulness and impact in each school, and perhaps in-service sessions for tapping the experience of other schools and of resource persons, seem necessary.

What emerges most significantly, however, are not the various ways in which the program falls short of its potential, but the fact that children and youth in Toronto's multi-faith schools are listening, thinking, appreciating, and are inwardly endorsing this aspect of their schooling which fosters their religious development. The possibilities of enlarging the proportion of such students are inviting.

Notes

[1]Cited in *Readings and Prayers for Use in Toronto Schools* (Board of Education for the City of Toronto, 1982), [p. ii]. All references, indicated henceforth in the text by page numbers in parentheses, are to this document. A new edition appeared in 1985 and is obtainable at $10.00 a copy from the Board of Education for the City of Toronto, 155 College Street, Toronto M5T 1P6.

5
Religious Study in the Regular Curriculum

A classical mode of fostering religious development in schools has been formal religious study, undertaken as part of the regular course-work prescribed by the school. *Prima facie,* the approach has much to recommend it. It acknowledges that the students' religious development deserves the same systematic attention given, for example, to their linguistic, literary and mathematical development. It can make a serious, continuing claim on students' time and effort, which is less likely to be the case with more incidental modes of religious education. The question, however, is whether this mode – practicable in schools identified with a particular denomination – remains feasible and useful in multi-faith schools.

Chapter 5 does not claim to offer a comprehensive answer to the question, but should enable readers to formulate an answer relevant to their own educational settings. An alternative approach is presented in Chapter 6, which describes optional religious study courses conducted by religious bodies and accommodated in the school's weekly schedule of classes.

Each approach is, at least in part, a reflection of a particular historical-legal relationship between religious bodies and the state. This particularity underscores the need to present, through this book, a diversity of case studies, each in its way illuminating, rather than a case for "the best way" of furthering religious development in multi-faith schools.

This report on religious study in the curriculum of Integrated schools in Newfoundland and Labrador is divided into four sections: structure and program; practice and effect – primary and elementary levels; practice and effect – junior and senior high levels; conclusions. It should be kept in mind that this does not purport to be a systematic survey or evaluation of a religious education program. As indicated, the case studies in this book have a different purpose – to suggest possibilities to educators seeking the appropriate role for their school(s) in the religious development of students.

Structure and Program

The structure of publicly funded schooling in Newfoundland and Labrador reflects the church-state partnership in education dating from the nineteenth century. Denominational superintendencies, each supported by public funds, were discontinued in the 1960s, but a multi-partite school system – Integrated, Pentecostal, Roman Catholic and Seventh Day Adventist – remains in place, now under a unified Department of Education. It is with one of these, the Integrated sector, that this study is concerned.

The Integrated Education Committee (recently renamed Council) dates from 1969, when the Anglican Church, the United Church and the Salvation Army formally merged their schools. Soon thereafter the Presbyterian Church became a fourth member, and in 1977 the Moravian Church was added. The Council thus serves five denominational groups, though the schools under its jurisdiction are even more diverse in their religious makeup.

Paralleled by similar structures in the Pentecostal, Roman Catholic and Seventh Day Adventist sectors, the Integrated Education Council is a publicly funded entity charged with various educational tasks under school law. These include: sharing in the formulation of provincial educational policy, establishing and dissolving Integrated school boards, distributing capital grants to those boards, participating in the licensing process for teachers in Integrated schools, and, in addition to a general responsibility to examine text materials in other subject areas, designing and revising curriculum in religious and family life education for Integrated schools. The Council comprises representatives of the constituent church bodies and the Integrated school boards, as well as an executive staff. Its Religious Education Committee, responsible for curriculum development, includes teachers, administrators and religious education coordinators from Integrated schools, as well as representatives of the denominations, the Newfoundland Department of Education, and the province's university (Memorial University), and one or more of the executive staff of the Council. The key channel of communication between the Committee and the religious education teachers dispersed throughout a large province is the twenty-one religious education coordinators. Informed of new policies and programs at semi-annual gatherings, they are responsible for their implementation by teachers, whose experience and needs are in turn represented to the Committee by the coordinators.

The aims of religious education in Integrated schools have been listed as follows by the Integrated Education Council:

1. To enable students to understand what religion, and in particular, Christianity, has contributed to our total way of life in the Western World.
2. To assist students in their understanding of what constitutes belief, what people believe and how their beliefs determine their behaviour and/or otherwise influence their lives.
3. To help students clarify their thinking on some of the fundamental questions about themselves and their relationship to other humans, to the universe, and to a transcendent order.
4. To help students develop for themselves an approach to life based on Christian principles. (It is more in keeping with the best in our religious traditions that a person be enabled to make the proper decisions than it is to have these decisions imposed by others).

Noticeably absent is any preoccupation with one or more denomination of Christianity. While the five constituent churches of the Council see to it that their positions are accurately conveyed in texts surveying Christian denominations, and not disparaged in expositions of the Christian way of life and its biblical and doctrinal bases, they do not expect the schools to provide any systematic education in their respective denominational principles.

The program designed to accomplish these aims is outlined below, as it existed in 1983-84. (Program revision is an important, continuing part of the work of the Integrated Religious Education Committee.)

Grades	Emphases and Materials
Primary Grades (Kindergarten and grades 1, 2 and 3)	Human relationships, and behavior consistent with the Christian view of man and of God. Extensive use is made of the DUSO program (Developing Understanding of Self and Others), along with texts depicting biblical and post-biblical examples of desirable human behavior.
Elementary Grades 4	The natural world and human life – their wonder and complexity – and the religious response of worship, stewardship, and so on. Text: *God's Ways in His World* (revised).
5 and 6	The Bible and its significance (Nature of scripture, chronology, biblical life and times). Texts: *Bible People and Bible Times – Old Testament* (Grade 5); *Bible People and Bible Times – New Testament* (Grade 6).
Junior High Grades (7, 8 and 9)	World religions, including Christianity, and the linkages with biblical concepts and history. Texts: *From Fear to Faith* (Grade 7); *Paths to Faith* (Grade 8); *Our Christian Heritage* (Grade 9).
High School Grades 10	Religious Education 1100. Contemporary life – relationships and communication, values styles, scientific outlook – and the significance of religion in life. Text: *The Dimensions of Religion* (revised).
11 and 12	Two streams, World Religions and Biblical, each comprising two courses. (1a) Religious Education 2100. Text: *Primitive and Eastern Religions.*

(1b) Religious Education 3100.
Text: *Western Religions*
(2a) Religious Education 2109
Text: *Old Testament: Its History, Culture and Themes.*
(2b) Religious Education 3109, New Testament.
Text: *A Doctor [Luke] Remembers.*

Every student, with the exceptions to be noted, follows this program from kindergarten to grade 9, and takes three or more of the five high school courses – normally, as indicated in the outline, RE 1100 in grade 10, and in grades 11 and 12 a choice from the remaining four courses. With regard to that choice, the Integrated Religious Education Committee sees advantages in staying within a stream – that is, taking the two World Religions or the two Biblical courses – but it has not established prerequisites or other regulations preventing any combination of courses. The Department of Education's requirement of a certain number of 3000-level courses for high school graduation, however, has some bearing on the student's choices.

Exemptions from part or all of the program are granted when parents so request on the grounds that it does not accord with their religious convictions or their views on religious education. This is the right of all parents, including members of the five denominations which sponsor the Integrated school system. Exemptions are also granted on parental request (with greater or lesser ease depending on the school board involved) to make room in a high school student's schedule for a needed course or courses. The number of "write-outs," as exemptions are called, is small in the two school boards visited. In one of the boards, of 255 grade 9 students being pre-registered in March for high school entry in September, 1984, only eleven students were "written out" of the religious education course, i.e., 4 percent, whereas some 20 percent of the student population of the board belonged to faiths other than the five Integrated denominations. Write-outs, of course, reflect parental perceptions, which do not necessarily match the true nature of the program. Two instances were mentioned of atheistic/agnostic parents who, on being informed that the program was descriptive rather than designed to nurture students as members of the faith community, rescinded their requests to have their children exempted.

Practice and Effect – Primary and Elementary Levels

An elementary school serving a number of small coastal communities is the main source of data for this section. Its enrollment of 262 students (1983-84) is religiously distributed as follows:

United Church	154
Anglican	55
Salvation Army	43
Roman Catholic	7
Other	3

The school's principal estimated that about one-half of these students take part in church life (that is, attend services and/or Sunday school). The "other" category includes Jehovah's Witnesses, whose families tend to request exemption from religious education. Though the only ones not participating, they are not, in the principal's experience, in any way ostracized by the other children.

According to a grade 1 teacher, students enjoy lessons based on the DUSO program. They respect the wise puppet-character, Duso, follow the stories attentively, and engage willingly in the prescribed activities, such as drawing, song, and role playing. The Religious Education Committee has chosen a series of Bible stories (Arch Books) to be used along with the DUSO lessons. With some exceptions, according to the teacher, the Bible stories are well matched to the children's age. Their correspondence with the DUSO lessons is grasped by the brighter children; for the other children they presumably serve to reinforce the lessons subconsciously. In the teacher's opinion, the Arch stories alone would not constitute a good religious education program for primary children.

The significance of the DUSO program and the Arch stories is explained in a Council document on the philosophy of primary religious education.

> DUSO helps the children reflect, at an elementary level, on such questions as "Who is my neighbour?" and "What is my responsibility to him?" "Am I my brother's keeper?" (p.9).
>
> DUSO speaks and deals with the child's humanity and for this reason it touches basic human concerns and questions. . . . Religious Education at this level should help children understand themselves and their relationship to others and generally to raise questions about human experiences. (p.9).
>
> The Arch Books . . . are obviously to be used as good little stories, and also as stories introducing the young children to selected Biblical characters, themes, parables, etc. But over and above these purposes . . . we intend them to be used to connect the real-life themes and experiences captured by the DUSO lessons with the real-life themes and experiences spoken to by the Bible. Though a meagre start, this kind of realistic use of Biblical materials should serve to encourage a positive, experiential

appreciation of not only the Bible itself but also religion and Religious
Education in general. It could be a small start in the direction away from
the view that religion is "merely a set of rules and pronouncements from
the Biblical position of a foreign time and place . . ." and toward the
realization that religion springs from the very act of living itself. (p. 12).

In grades 5 and 6, as indicated earlier, the Bible becomes the focus of attention, but not as an object of purely academic interest, detached from the
student's imagination. Thus, in one grade 5 lesson, a chapter of the text was
read describing the exile in Babylon as experienced by a Jewish merchant.
A similar appeal to the imagination was apparent in a forthcoming writing
assignment – a description of the feelings of a Jew returning to Jerusalem
from exile, and of the feelings of a Jew deciding to stay in Babylon.

The program also attempts to relate biblical material to the student's
own life. For example, the teacher's guide accompanying the grade 5 text
stipulates these objectives for Chapter 2, "The Twin Brothers" (Esau and
Jacob):

To help students understand

– that conflict can exist in different personalities and within a family
– the importance of love and forgiveness
– the significance of the birthright and blessing in partriarchal times.

The combination of biblical knowledge and contemporary applications is
also apparent in the guide's suggestion that "poems of thanks could be
created by students – to God for the Ten Commandments – after discussing
how important it is to have order and discipline in a society – our society."

Biblical events in themselves, without imaginative overlay or application, evidently also hold interest for students. A grade 6 teacher mentioned
his class' interest in the topic of the crucifixion. The principal (who teaches
religious education in grade 5) told of a student's favorable reaction on
learning that the Israelites' Red Sea crossing may be interpreted in more
than one way: "I couldn't understand how that happened [before]." Other
biblical events that intrigue students are apparent in these questions, reported
by another grade 5 teacher: did the flood cover the whole earth? were Adam
and Eve the first people?

The principal noted that he is careful to point out to the students that he
is not casting doubt on the truth of the Bible. The opening of new perspectives on scripture – without claiming for them any indisputable validity –
does not, in his view, hurt faith or confuse children; rather, it makes for a
more solid faith.

The impression that religious education is meaningful for many students
is reinforced by written responses from a grade 5 and a grade 6 class. In an
attempt to tap something of the deeper, more internalized effect of religious
education, I composed brief stories illustrating religious awareness or consciousness and religious knowledge. Having heard a story, the students were
asked to identify sources of the protagonist's religious consciousness and
knowledge.

The story used in the grade 5 class went as follows:

> It was a clear night, and the sky was filled with stars, wonderfully bright and close. Pat stood in the darkness outside the house and looked and looked. As Pat stood gazing in wonder, this thought came into Pat's head: Glory to God.
> How had Pat learned to think a thought like that?
> Had anyone ever helped Pat to think thoughts like that? Had religious education lessons at school helped Pat to think thoughts like that?

After the students had responded to those questions, the story continued:

> Lying in bed that night, Pat remembered how God created stars and so much besides. First there was nothing, just emptiness; then, step by step God caused sky and earth to be, sun and moon and stars, dry land and the oceans, all kinds of trees and vegetation, fish, birds, and animals, and lastly man and woman. Then God, looking upon what he had created, said: "It is very, very good."
> Where had Pat most likely learned about God creating everything step by step and then saying how good it was? At home? At church? At Sunday School? At regular school in religious education lessons?

The students were told that they could choose more than one alternative, as well as add others.

The following table quantifies responses to the first set of questions, under the heading,"Consciousness;" and to the second set, under the heading, "Knowledge."

Grade 5 Students' Perceptions of Sources of Consciousness and Knowledge of God as Creator

	Consciousness	Knowledge
Number of students responding	18	18
Number responding comprehensibly	15	18
Sources		
Home	2 (13%)	2 (11%)
Church[a]	6 (40%)	11 (61%)
Sunday School	4 (27%)	12 (67%)
Religious Education	10 (67%)	7 (39%)
Other Specified Sources	3 (20%)	

[a]includes responses such as "minister" and "priest."

The results suggest that religious education at school has, for a significant proportion of students, been a source of awareness and knowledge of God's creative action in the universe. The smaller number (39%) affirming religious education as a source of detailed knowledge of the biblical account of creation probably reflects program emphasis: the grade 4 program, while treating the universe as God's handiwork, does not dwell on the story of creation as found in Genesis; the grade 5 program, in turn, takes up other portions of the Old Testament.

A different story was presented to the grade 6 class, but the questions remained the same. In brief, Pat is cruelly teased by a classmate and yet shows consideration when that classmate needs a ride home one day, because Pat recalls the idea: love those who treat you unkindly. In the second half of the story, Pat recalls details of Jesus' relationship with the religious leaders of his day, and his forgiveness of them as he hung on the cross. The students' responses are tabulated as follows:

Grade 6 Students' Perceptions of Sources of Consciousness and Knowledge of Christ-like Love for Enemies

	Consciousness	Knowledge
Number of Students Responding	25	25
Number Responding Comprehensibly	21	23
Sources		
Home[a]	14 (67%)	10 (43%)
Church[b]	15 (71%)	22 (96%)
Sunday School	3 (14%)	19 (83%)
Religious Education[c]	21 (100%)	22 (96%)
Other Specified Sources	7 (33%)	1 (4%)

Notes: [a]Includes: "parents," "father," "mother"
[b]Includes: "minister"
[c]Includes the responses: "school" and "teacher(s)" (4 responses in all)

The significance of religious education is suggested even more strongly by the grade 6 data than by the grade 5 responses. The particular religious content referred to in the story probably accounts for this difference, for the grade 6 religious education program, as apparently also the other sources listed in the table, focuses directly on the life and message of Jesus. One respondent brings out clearly the parallel influence of the various agencies:

> Pat learned about Jesus in all of the places because at home she might have had a bible, at church the minister would read about it, at Sunday School they would be taught about it, and in regular school in Religious Education lessons they learn from the Bible but in a different book and in different words. [Writing errors corrected.]

The evidence thus far assembled indicates that religious education on the Newfoundland Integrated model can be a meaningful part of schooling for children through the elementary years. Whether the program also registers with older students is the next question.

Practice and Effect – Junior and Senior High Levels

This section includes data on one of the junior high years and on some courses of the high school program. A school in a suburban community, enrolling 800 students, was the setting for the grade 7 class visited. The school board's religious education coordinator estimated that 60 percent of the students are Anglican – many of them nominal – with most of the remainder belonging to the United Church and to denominations other than the five Integrated churches.

The particular grade 7 class included five Roman Catholics and a member of the Faith sect among its 25 or so students. Of these six students, two Roman Catholics take part in the religious education program; the other four students have been "written out" by their parents. They do other work at their desks during religious education lessons, but may occasionally become involved in the discussion, as when the boy belonging to the Faith sect spoke up during my dialogue with the class. The teacher reported that exempted students are no less accepted socially by their classmates than the majority who take religious education.

The teacher considers religious education to be workable and worthwhile. It engages the students by its openness and encouragement to discussion, and yet is not lacking in substance. Students have likened it to history, and, indeed, it serves as a reinforcement of that subject. Along with other subjects, it contributes to the development of values. Teaching religious education, and being able to consult with a colleague who is a minister of religion, have fed the teacher's motivation to teach the subject.

The lesson observed began with a review of the beliefs and customs of various pre-industrial societies regarding birth and death. The students were reasonably responsive to the teacher's questions. Their participation was perhaps more marked during the body of the lesson, which dealt with baptism as practiced by various denominations. Students reported on the rite they themselves had undergone, some with much specific detail, even to the point of quoting words of the rite. The teacher ably supplemented information they furnished and also qualified some of their observations. The following exchange is illustrative:

T   What is the purpose of baptism?
S1 To enter the Kingdom of God.
T   Yes, that is what some people believe.
S2 To give you a name.
T   It is not really necessary for that, because a name can be given when the birth is registered.

Thanks to the teacher's tone and manner, students could feel secure; she was not belittling their religious knowledge but, through her commentary, enlarging and refining it.

In their conversation with me, the class offered further evidence that religious education extends the religious horizons of students. Though able to recall few specific lessons from earlier years of religious education, some have distinct memories of a visit to a synagogue. Those students currently involved in educational programs at their churches – a small minority according to the show of hands – see religious education in grade 7 as very different from the Jesus and Bible-centred church instruction.

The class was given the hypothetical case of the need to reduce the length of the school day to conserve energy. A subject would have to be dropped from the curriculum. Which one should it be? Suggestions, solicited from class members individually, ran the gamut, but only one student proposed religious education. Deference to the feelings of the teacher probably did not create a bias in favor of religious education because, being responsible for several subjects, the teacher is not identified with religious education in particular. The lighter demands of religious education in comparison with, say, mathematics, may have been a biasing factor, but one can probably allow for it and still be left with a substantial vote of confidence for religious education.

At the high school level, religious education teachers were interviewed at two institutions – one in the suburban district containing the junior high school just referred to, the other in the coastal district containing the elementary school described earlier. The interviews revealed that religious education enjoys student acceptance in grades 10 to 12 as it does in the lower grades.

One teacher, whose time is almost exclusively taken up with religious education, noted that few of his students are church-goers but almost all display a positive attitude towards his subject. Another teacher, whose assignment comprises English as well as religious education, remarked that students show equal interest in both subjects. Negativism – "Why do we have to do this?" – is as likely to be expressed towards English or physics or any other subject as it is towards religious education. A third teacher reported that a number of graduates embarking on teaching careers have chosen religious education as their subject specialty.

I observed two lessons, one in the New Testament course (3109), the other in the western world religions course (3100). Both teachers showed a strong grasp of their subject, both were enthusiastic and dynamic, and yet the students did not exhibit a corresponding eagerness or spontaneity. Does this passivity contradict the teachers' claims regarding student attitudes towards religious education? Not really, according to a religious education co-ordinator. While enjoying parity of esteem with other courses, religious education is also like them in respect to teaching style and student response. Exposition of subject matter by the teacher, and listening and/or note-taking by students, appear to be the dominant modes in the high schools. An interview with a small group of students confirmed that few students become involved in class discussions in religious education courses; more students may be enjoying the subject but, as in other courses, do not speak up due to shyness; another group attends and listens, but with little real interest –

again, as occurs in other courses.

If this characterization is true of the high school religious education program as a whole, it appears least applicable to the Grade 10 course, because of the interest RE1100 awakens among many students. The course is an exploration of contemporary life and values, including explicitly religious phenomena, with attention to their worth from a Christian point of view. Students discover that religion is not limited to church-going, but is implicated in many human activities and concerns. The topics lend themselves well to discussion (but not to formal testing, said two teachers). A sense of freedom to engage in one's own search is present: the Christian perspective is disclosed but not imposed. For all these reasons, this is the course students like best and teachers "love to teach," according to a number of teachers and students.

The textbook itself[1] makes for interesting reading. It is an anthology of readings as diverse as "St. Paul's Ideas on Love" (1 Corinthians 13:1-13) and "Housewife mother vs working father – whose job is tougher?" Articles deal with such intriguing subjects as extrasensory perception and reincarnation; puzzles and other challenging activities exhibit the nature of scientific and religious knowledge. In many instances, without denying the interest or, very often, the solid wisdom of the selection, the unassisted reader must wonder how it relates to religion, whether conceived as formal religion or "ultimate concern." For those readings, sociology, psychology, human values, and the like, seem to be apter categories than religion. The student-reader, however, has the teacher to help situate the readings in a religious perspective. This is easily done where the problems and possibilities of human relationships are the topic, for they represent the practical side of the religious injunction to love one's neighbor.

Another course which stands out among the high school religious education offerings is the New Testament course (3109). It is true that observation of a session of the course did not reveal an animated response on the part of many students. Conversations with a small group of students in each school, however, suggested that for some students at least, the course "connects" well with other facets of their religious experience and growth. One gave the example of the gospel account of the multiplication of loaves and fishes by Jesus. Studied in the course, it carried greater meaning when heard again in church. Another expressed it this way: "Students can get a lot out of the New Testament course – it's meaningful; it presents the New Testament in a light they can understand." A student's remark cited by a teacher – "It's all beginning to make sense now" – points up the relevance of the course to the student's existing, but confused, stock of religious ideas. The growth in enrollment in the course at one school – from two sections in 1982-83 to four in 1983-84 – corroborates the students' comments.

The course text, *A Doctor Remembers*[2], tells the history of Jesus and of the early Christian church as recorded by the physician-evangelist, St. Luke. The events are brought to life not merely by vivid touches, historical details, and contemporary references, but by reflections on their meaning in the light of Christian scholarship. Without over-simplifying, or subordinating content to "relevance" to the concerns of today's youth, the author engages the reader's interest, imagination, and mind. (In the introduction to the book he states that "at every stage of its production I have sat in my imagination beside those who will be using it. The needs and interests of senior high school students and their teachers have been constantly in my thoughts." [p. X])

A Doctor Remembers, though reflective and well-grounded in scholarship, does not assume a neutral stance regarding its subject, if that were possible. The author does not conceal what he sees as valuable and important for humanity. Thus, while much of the text reads "neutrally," its overall tone and specific passages invite an endorsement by the reader. The following passage can serve as an example; it provides factual information which detracts from the uniqueness of Jesus, but it also conveys the conviction that Jesus is not just one among many parable-tellers.

> Jesus did not invent the method of teaching by parables. In his day rabbis used parables to explain the meaning of Old Testament passages. There are parables in the Old Testament itself, for example Nathan's powerful story of the poor man's ewe lamb with which he confronted King David and rebuked his sin (II Samuel 12). In using parables Jesus was following a method of communicating truth which had already been found effective, and which his hearers would recognize. But he used this medium of expression in his own inimitable way. No teacher ever used parables so effectively. (p. 47)

Religious education also may enter the realm of a high school student's life-choices through personal communication between teacher and student. One non-clerical teacher said: "Students will open up to you outside of class; you've hit on something that's inside them." Two clergymen-teachers said that students engage them in private dialogue, one noting, in reply to the question whether such dialogue is a function of the teacher's personality rather than subject, that his religious education students, not his English students, seek it. The phenomenon is not an inevitable part of the religious education teacher's role, however, for one non-clerical teacher indicated that, in contrast with his clergyman-colleague, it did not occur in his case.

Conclusions

The Newfoundland Integrated religious education program, as depicted in this case study, illustrates a worthwhile role for the school in the religious development of students differing in religious persuasion. In this conclusion, that role is briefly characterized and evaluated, and its supporting conditions described.

Wide acceptability is one of the program's salient characteristics. The program serves not only the students belonging to five diverse Christian denominations – Anglicans, Moravians, Presbyterians, United Church and

Salvation Army – but most of those belonging to other denominations and attending Integrated schools. The right of conscientious exemption is not exercised by a significant proportion of Roman Catholics and even by some Jehovah's Witnesses, although both those religious bodies have traditionally manifested a strong sense of their own identity vis à vis other Christian churches.

The religious diversity of the audience is even greater than the denominational labels suggest. With few exceptions, each group embraces a broad range of faith and practice, from close adherence to the beliefs of the church and regular church attendance, to a meager awareness of the beliefs and no active connection with the church whatever. Even parents of atheistic or agnostic persuasion have in some instances asked that their children be enrolled, on learning that the program is not intended to promote adherence to the Christian faith.

A second hallmark, then, is complementarity – the program does not copy the formation in faith dispensed by family and church, and yet it bolsters that formation. In the early years it develops the personal and interpersonal awareness and behavior that are implicit in the Christian view of man. In the middle and later years of schooling, the program expands students' intellectual understanding of religion and of Christianity so that, to use an analogy that arose in an interview with students, religious education becomes a "ladder out of babyhood" – one is not kept at the Bible-story level. And yet, this complementarity is based on a difference of emphasis between religious education at school and religious formation at home and church. The comments of grade 5 and 6 students even suggest that at certain levels in the program, there is as much reinforcement as complementarity. That is, church and school are engaged to a considerable degree in imparting the same knowledge and the same religious consciousness. A degree of reinforcement is also apparent in the high school New Testament course, which, while probably vastly extending the student's knowledge of Christianity, also reinforces the invitation to faith which a student might well hear in church.

Does it work? Is the Integrated religious education program having the desired impact on students? The data suggest that: religious education is a meaningful part of the curriculum, enjoying at least the same interest and response on the part of students as any other subject; certain parts of the program (specifically the DUSO-based curriculum in the youngest grades and the grade 10 course on contemporary life and values and their religious significance) strongly interest many students; courses dealing with the Bible genuinely advance the religious understanding of some students, clarifying confusion and contradictions in their existing stock of religious ideas. It also appears that religious education may prompt students to talk privately with religious education teachers about matters affecting their own lives.

The framework within which these goals are achieved can be described under three headings: teachers, community, and Council.

A corps of religious education teachers – specialists to varying degrees in grades 7 or 8 and upwards, and all-subject teachers in the lower grades – has emerged, feeling confidence and satisfaction in their efforts in religious education. Prior to Integration in 1969, there was no clearly articulated and recognized role for teachers in this subject area. Religious education was not offered in all schools, and typically lacked careful definition and organization. It also carried the stigma of being a church enterprise rather than an educational one. The pioneering educator-clergyman in developments since 1969, A.B. LeGrow, wrote:

> In the first years after Integration, I met with some 3,200 teachers in small groups, mainly to acquaint teachers with the nature of the Religious Education programs and our supposed philosophy and approach. At first, many teachers were apprehensive that the Church was trying to push something down their throats. It took some time to allay those fears and to overcome apathy and even hostility with acceptance or at worst, neutrality.[3]

Success in the classroom, coupled with continuing inservice work, and increasing pre-service specialization in religion and religious education, will likely further strengthen the competence and confidence of the teachers. To these influences can perhaps be added: (1) the religious motivation of many teachers – in one of the schools visited, a teacher estimated that 31 of the 35 staff members could be termed devout Christians, a figure, however, which a religious education coordinator in another board considered high; (2) the importance of references from clergy in the awarding of licenses to prospective teachers in Integrated schools; and (3) a sense of contractual obligation to accept an assignment in religious education, given the church-related character of the Integrated school system.

Implicit in the foregoing is the support, often indirect, lent to religious education by the community. The common practice of daily opening exercises and occasional special services represents the endorsement of a religious orientation of education by teachers, parents, school boards, and clergy. The province's Department of Education, too, can be ranked among these, for the official *Aims of Public Education for Newfoundland and Labrador* states:

> We believe that one who has achieved his fullest and best development as an individual is one who, to the best of his ability,
> i) Is possessed of a religious faith as maintained and taught by the church of his affiliation, and
> ii) Is possessed of a sense of moral values, based on a belief, and an earnest endeavour to practice and exemplify in his daily living the virtues, both spiritual and moral, affirmed by his religious faith.

The third factor in the viability and impact of religious education in the Integrated schools is the Integrated Education Council, and specifically its Religious Education Committee. Established on a sound legislative and financial basis, and with a clear sense of its purpose, the Committee has been a strong but gentle mover and shaker in religious education. It is difficult to know how the developments of the past fifteen years could have occurred, and how continued growth can occur, without the intelligent and prudent leadership of those constituting or acting for the Committee.

Notes

[1] Murray Randell and Ross Reccord, Eds., *The Dimensions of Religion,* Revised Edition (St. John's, Newfoundland: Integrated Education Committee, 1979).

[2] John B. Corston, *A Doctor Remembers,* Third edition (Scarborough, Ontario: Nelson Canada, 1983).

[3] A.B. LeGrow, "Where Have We Come and What Are We Doing," *Religious Education for the 80's: Implications for the Student.* Proceedings of a colloguium sponsored by the Integrated Education Committee and the Religious Education Committee, St. Bride's College, Littledale, Newfoundland, November 7-9, 1979, p. 45.

6
Elective Religious Study in an Elementary/Junior High School

At the heart of the various case studies contained in this book lies the question of whether schools with a religiously mixed staff and student body can and ought to contribute to students' religious development. Arguments against such a role for the school include the claims that religious development, if it is to mean anything, must occur within a believing community, such as a church or synagogue; that religious education militates against the integration of the diverse religious groups in the school; that schools are institutions of secular education and must not be charged with the functions of religious institutions.

This chapter intends not to comprehensively assess such claims, but to describe one situation where a worthwhile contribution to religious development is being made by a multi-faith school without compromising the school's other functions.

To clarify our working definitions, religious development means the student's growth in knowledge of, and responsiveness to, that which is of deepest meaning and value in human existence; religious education refers to all school practices intended to foster such growth; and religious study, i.e., formal courses on religion, is just one of the many approaches to religious education.

This report has four sections: a general description of the school's provisions for religious education, with particular attention to religious study; an evaluation of the provisions by persons in administrative roles; religious education in action – a description and evaluation by teachers and students and on the basis of my direct observation; and finally, conclusions.

Religious Education Provisions in General

Bridge Street School[1] is part of the public school system of Halifax, Nova Scotia. The school board has promulgated regulations governing religious study in its elementary and junior high schools. Religious instruction is permissible as part of the weekly class schedule if parents and religious bodies take responsibility for curriculum and staffing, and subject to agreement being reached between them and the school principal. (The regulations also provide for an alternative, the scheduling of religious instruction outside of school hours.) Time ceilings are established for religious instruction given within school hours, and students not attending the religion classes are to have "appropriate constructive activities" arranged for them by the school staff.

At Bridge Street School, two groups have availed themselves of the option to offer religious study: a Roman Catholic parish and a group of Protestant churches located within walking distance of the school. All the churches concerned are members of an area ecumenical council, which endorses and offers token financial support to the two programs. Endorsement is also given by the Bridge Street School Parent-Teacher Association, which makes an small, annual financial contribution. The Protestant program, which involves no salaried administrative position, can be maintained through this funding and through the donation of learning materials by some of the sponsoring Protestant churches. The major source of funding for the Roman Catholic program is parish monies, gathered mainly through Sunday collections.

The teaching staff for religious study classes at Bridge Street School is entirely volunteer, recruited by the (salaried) director of religious education of the Roman Catholic parish and by a volunteer co-ordinator who acts on behalf of the Protestant churches. The historical situation in which a teaching appointment at Bridge Street School (then attended and staffed only by Roman Catholics) automatically entailed the teaching of religion, no longer obtains. In 1983-84 there were eight teachers for the Protestant program – three of them members of the full-time school staff, and five recruited from the community; there were twenty-four teachers for the Roman Catholic program – eleven of them on staff, and thirteen recruited externally.

The curriculum used by the Roman Catholic religious study classes is, in most cases, the Canadian Catechism, a program for grades 1 to 8 authorized by the Canadian Catholic bishops. Far from being a catechism in the traditional sense of questions and answers about the faith, it seeks to integrate the experience of the learners with the biblical perspective, beliefs and practices of Christians; distinctively Roman Catholic elements are present but not dominant, and there is a measure of integration between the program and the initiation of children into the sacramental life of the church, particularly in relation to preparation for First Communion and Penance. Protestant classes do not have a corresponding graded program; their diverse curricula, reflecting teacher choice, tend to give much attention to the Bible and the life of Jesus and avoid content distinctive of one or another Protestant denomination.

At the start of each school year parents are asked to indicate on a form whether they wish their child enrolled in Roman Catholic religious study, Protestant religious study, or a supervised study period. The parallel options are scheduled at the same time each week – on Mondays for the youngest grades, Wednesdays for the intermediate grades, and Fridays for the junior high school grades (7-9). The numbers in the three categories in 1983-84 follow:

Roman Catholic Religious Study 349
Protestant Religious Study   154
Supervised Study Sessions   233
                                   ———
Total school enrollment   736

(Figures as of the end of January, 1984)

In addition to the opportunity for weekly religious study, Bridge Street School gives students a daily experience of prayer, as the school day starts with the principal reciting the Lord's Prayer over the public address system, followed by the playing of "O Canada." There are also special events incorporating a religious element, such as the grade 9 graduation ceremony and the Christmas concert.

Administrators' Evaluation of Religious Education Provisions

The administrators referred to in this section are the person in charge of the Roman Catholic program – the previously mentioned director of religious education of the Roman Catholic parish; the coordinator of the Protestant program; and the principal and vice-principal of Bridge Street School.

The Roman Catholic director believes that the religious study classes make a worthwhile contribution to faith development. In the absence of the program, she estimates that forty to fifty percent of the students would lack effective access to the Christian message. For them the program is a link with the church, that is, with people openly committed to the Christian faith and community. The concern their religion teachers have for them constitutes a "powerful message" that might later open the way for their own participation in the Christian community. For the other students also – the fifty to sixty percent who participate in church life – religious study at school has a positive impact, in the director's estimation.

Nevertheless, in her view the in-school program has its limitations. Its efficacy with students at the junior high level is less than with the younger students. For those who came forward to enroll, an out-of-school program would have a greater impact on faith development. It would entail a greater measure of participation on the part of the students' families than the school program, which, strictly speaking, requires only a checkmark by a parent on a form once a year. An out-of-school program, whether conducted in people's homes or in church facilities (or, for that matter, in a school building after hours or on weekends) would necessitate some direct link between parents and church, as well as the weekly exercise of a conscious parental option in seeing that their children attended religion class. Parental involvement could well exceed that minimum, since an out-of-school program offers considerable opportunity for parental participation, as is the case, for example, with the current Confirmation course run by the parish. In that course four couples work with the director in teaching, and all parents potentially take part in a number of the sessions, rather as co-learners with their teenaged children.

The director noted another, albeit lesser, limitation of the in-school program, namely, its relatively late start in the school year. The October start makes religious study appear as an "extra," added on to the regular school program, which commences in the first days of September.

On the other hand, her role as director of Roman Catholic religious study enjoys general acceptance in the school, as demonstrated by the friendly respect shown her by administration and teachers. There is satisfaction, she senses, that the program is run well, without stresses or onerous responsibilities for school personnel.

A perennial challenge faced by the director is that of maintaining a full contingent of volunteer teachers and substitutes for the Roman Catholic classes. Automatic participation by internal teachers has ceased, with the result that over half the volunteers now must be recruited from outside the school. With the increase of female employment away from home during school hours, that recruitment becomes more difficult.

The Protestant co-ordinator's experience with the Protestant religious study program at Bridge Street School corresponds rather closely with that of her Roman Catholic counterpart.[2] She too remarked on the difficulty of staff recruitment – severe enough to prevent the mounting of a Grade 7 and 8 Protestant religious study class in 1983-84; she shared the sense of cooperation from administration and teachers, particularly since, in taking the role, she relieved the school principal of some of the program's administrative burdens; and she held the view that a large proportion of those enrolled in the Protestant religious study program – sixty percent is her estimate – would not otherwise receive any religious instruction.

The co-ordinator regards the program as necessary because each part of the child must be nurtured, the spiritual as well as the mental, the two being inseparable; she believes this to be true whatever the child's faith. The children she serves are nurtured in the basics of the Christian message and are encouraged but not coerced to attend their own church. Stated differently, her purpose is "to bring God and Jesus out of the Bible so that they become part of the child's life. . . . God is not just part of a story in a book, but real, alive and influential in the lives of children."

The principal and vice-principal of Bridge Street School see the religious study programs in the same light – as providing some basic Christian upbringing, and contributing in some measure to church attendance. It has even happened that parents choose to return to the church when their children become involved in its life. The administrators confirmed the view of the Roman Catholic director and the Protestant co-ordinator that the lack of a school religious study program would deprive some children of religious instruction entirely, but they did not suggest what percentage of children would be so affected.

One of the program's strengths, according to the two administrators, is the involvement of external teachers. When students see the parent of a fellow student coming to the school to teach religion, they experience a powerful lesson in the living of one's faith; internal religion teachers are less likely to have that impact, since they are seen as belonging to the school and fulfilling part of their institutional role.

One limitation perceived by the principal and vice-principal is an underemphasis on doctrine in the Roman Catholic program – "humanism is the accent." Another limitation, suggested by the principal, is that occasioned by an "anti-religious" phase in students' development in the junior high years. Unless the teacher can respond sensitively, there is risk of losing the gains of the earlier years of religious study. The fact that five junior high students had transferred from the supervised study option to religious study by mid-January of the 1983-84 year, while fewer had transferred out of religious study, perhaps indicates that the junior high religion teachers are responding appropriately to the challenge.

The administrators also briefly assessed other forms of religious education at the Bridge Street School. The daily prayer signifies to the students the importance of prayer, and is an opportunity to start the school day "on the right foot." The religious element of the graduation program, including readings and singing by students, and an address by a clergyman, is valued by the students. Objections have been raised by a few parents, but are not representative of the great majority of families. However, there have been occasions when, in the principal's view, the invited speaker dwelled on religious themes to excess, giving grounds on which parents might have objected.

Religious Education in Action

The testimony of both religion teachers and students and my own observations corroborate the assessments of the administrators, while also disclosing some differences worth noting.

The teacher of the Roman Catholic primary class (children aged five and six) feels constrained by time and numbers: at the primary level, only twenty minutes per week are available for religious study, and there are thirty children in the class. (The Protestant co-ordinator had reported that no Protestant primary course is offered because, in her view, the brevity of time would impose an unreasonable onus on a teacher.) A daily religion period, as during the time when the school enrolled Roman Catholics almost exclusively, would be a pedagogically superior arrangement, according to the primary teacher.

Given the time constraints, the course must dispense with pupil activities other than listening and responding verbally to stories told by the teacher with the aid of illustrated books. The subject matter is generally drawn from the life of Jesus. The children are receptive and enthusiastic; for many of them this is a new experience, as they have not previously been told of Jesus and, for instance, of the connection between Jesus and Christmas. For those with prior knowledge, the course serves as a worthwhile and appreciated reinforcement, for at this age level particularly, what is heard from the teacher takes on a special significance.

Children in the course receive encouragement to attend church in the form of the example of their peers and suggestions by the teacher that they ask a family member to take them to church. A parent had confided to the teacher that her child had come home and said he wanted to go to Mass, with the result that the parents now attend Mass regularly with the child. For many of the children, however, the course is probably their only source of information about the Christian faith. Were such a course not available, the teacher doubts that they would be sent to out-of-school religious instruction.

The daily recitation of the "Our Father" represents an additional means of religious education, whether or not the students are enrolled in the religious study course. Hearing the prayer each day, they gradually become able to join in its recitation. At times the teacher develops a discussion from the prayer – noting, for example, God's providence in relation to "our daily bread" – but does so with a little apprehension because of the possibility of parental objections.

The grade 1 Protestant class, taught by the Protestant co-ordinator, does not suffer from the constraints of time and numbers noted in the Roman Catholic primary class. Ten children are enrolled, and effective instructional time is at least fifty minutes. It was thus possible, in the lesson I observed, to add a coloring activity, singing, and a demonstration (a blindfolded child guided by a classmate), to the reading[3] of the textbook and questioning by the teacher.

The textbook uses two fictional children, six-year old Simon and five-year old Sarah, as a vehicle for teaching about God, Jesus and biblical figures, and encouraging Christian moral conduct and the practice of prayer. For example, the book shows a family watching television and having this conversation:

"Look at those mountains," said Simon, staring at the television screen.
"I wouldn't like to climb those without a guide!" said Daddy.
"What's a guide?" asked Sarah.

Daddy's response to Sarah's question leads to a short exposition of God's guidance in life. "He will be our Guide forever" (Psa. 48:14) is quoted, and the lesson concludes with a prayer: "Thank You, God, for being with us wherever we go. Amen." With the aid of the textbook, the teacher seeks to ensure that the children understand the meaning of the day's prayer before they actually pray.

The children's attention fluctuated during the observed session. For instance, the reading and explaining of the textbook selection, dealing with John the Baptist's role as a messenger preparing people for the coming of Jesus, did not command the same attention as the singing and "signing" by gestures, of a song, "Jesus loves me, this I know, because the Bible tells me so. . . ." The importance of the active in the pedagogy of this age group seems evident. Nevertheless, the children also showed the capacity and interest to respond to a thought-prompting question: why would a mother or father not give a child what the child asks for? Their responses were mature, and, as the teacher intended, provided a good basis for understanding her point that we do not always receive what we ask for in prayer.

The grade 2 Protestant teacher provided some further evidence that children take an interest in religious study – they talk about it at home, as the Roman Catholic primary teacher also reported (see above). The aim of the grade 2 teacher is not merely to help children know but also to do: thus, it is not enough to know a Bible story about, say, forgiveness; one must be able, through the help of Jesus, to forgive. Certain sayings from Scripture are memorized by the children so that they may "have the word in their hearts." It is not surprising that instruction aimed at doing and feeling, as well as knowing, should register with the students to the point of their talking about religion at home.

For about half of eighteen or so children enrolled each year, this religious study class at school is the principal opportunity for religious learning, since their families maintain no regular contact with a church. The teacher mentioned the ignorance of religion manifested by such students. For the other half of the group, the program is also worthwhile as a reinforcement and enrichment of what they learn in Sunday School.

In her full-time capacity, the teacher is responsible for one of the grade 1 classes of Bridge Street School. She reported that the daily recitation of the Lord's Prayer is well received by the pupils, who show reverence and join in saying the words. The school Christmas concert is another opportunity for religious learning, as more than half of its content has a religious theme (a proportion which, the teacher speculated, reflects the judgement that children are well exposed through the environment to the secular themes of Christmas). Incidental religious education also occurs in the course of daily class work, typically resulting from a student's comment. A child may assert, in a discussion about animals, that "God made the animals that way." In such a case, the teacher would reinforce the child's belief, while conscious that in speaking of religion in the regular classroom she might be "stepping on toes."

The reader's attention is now directed to the upper grades in the school. The Roman Catholic grade 9 lesson I observed dealt with the meaning of some of the Commandments, chiefly through exposition by the teacher and frequent elicitation of student response. Concreteness of imagery and examples, however, was notable in the lesson and undoubtedly added to the students' attentiveness. For example, each of the nineteen students was called on individually to answer the question: how do you honor your father and mother? Then the teacher gave a thoroughly realistic rendition of what "hassling" a parent might sound like. The teacher also, however, turned the searchlight on herself, by describing some of the ways in which she, an adult, continues to honor her parent. A graphic, future lesson on the next commandment, "You shall not kill," was predictable as the session drew to a close in roughly this manner:

The teacher wrote the commandment on the board, along with a summary of its intent: "Human life, in its beginning, continuance and end, is primarily the domain of (is to be controlled by) God." Then she said, "How many expect to kill somebody in the course of their life?" That numbing question was followed by the identification of possible circumstances entailing the taking of life: self-defense, war, the protection of property, an accident, euthanasia, abortion. The teacher ended the lesson with instructions to the girls: "Try to imagine this situation: you are the victim of rape and you discover two months later that you are pregnant. What's the right thing to do?" And for the boys: "Your mother is in hospital, in a coma, a vegetable, but waking occasionally and screaming in pain. What should you do?"

The class disbanded. In the hallway, some boys were already talking about the situation put to them, and were being asked by a friend, not a member of the religion class, where the question had come up.

When interviewed, the teacher described the school as primarily concerned with the knowledge dimension of religious development; values and feelings could more effectively be addressed by church and home. The lesson showed the teacher's concern with knowledge and thought, but also suggested that in her teaching, cognition is not divorced from valuing and feeling. Another teacher, responsible for a grade 8 Roman Catholic class, commented on students' desire to "open up" regarding their feelings on religion. Normally restrained by peer pressure, they see religion class as a place to do so safely, particularly since the teacher is prepared to reveal her own feelings. Her course comprises a study of the sacraments. Along with facts, attitudes are imparted; she suggests to students that they look upon weekly attendance at the Eucharist as giving back to God one hour of the 168 hours of life God gives them. Some students have developed the habit of church attendance as a result of the religious study course.

A direct opportunity to tap students' thinking on religion and religious education came in a grade 9 Protestant class. Responding to my questions, students stated that without religious study they would not be as knowledgeable about God and the Bible, about "whom to turn to." This would be true, they felt, whether or not they were receiving religious instruction from family and church. Religious study, however, is not the only way in which school stimulates their thinking about the deeper questions of life. Teachers of other subjects have had that effect, as, for example when a careers teacher asked, "What are you going to do with your life?" The teachers, too, may speak convincingly about showing consideration for fellow students in the course of "secular" class work.

The daily prayer at Bridge Street School received mixed reactions. While some of the students seemed satisfied with the prevailing setting and form, others voiced these criticisms: "not the right atmosphere;" "the exact same thing every day;" (paraphrased) not what you might want to pray about; "a quiet time would allow individuals to refer to what's on their mind in prayer." (The Roman Catholic grade 9 teacher noted that the students are respectful during the prayer, but with the exception of four or five in a classroom, do not join in. This changes decidedly when the prayer is being offered for an individual, say, a fellow student who has suffered an accident; then the fervor is very apparent.)

In a Roman Catholic grade 7 class, students were asked: "What should a person learn in order to be a real member of the Christlike family [i.e., the people of all eras who, whether Christians or not, attempt to live as Christ taught]?" Results were as follows, in descending order of frequency (noted in parentheses and with illustrative responses):

- Selfless love (16)
  "Learn to love his enemies just as family and friends"
  "Kind and sharing"
  "What it means to be forgiven and how to forgive."
- Church attendance (6)
  "Go to church and understand why they are there"
- Christ (5)
  "Learn how Christ was like"
- God (4)
  "Learn about God, about the part God plays in our lives"
- Appreciativeness (3)
  "Appreciate what he has and not be greedy"
- Being like God (2)
  "Live in [God's] image"
- Involvement (2)
  "Take an active part in the Christlike family"
- Commandments (2)
  "Follow the Ten Commandments"

The other categories of response had a frequency of one.

Conclusions

These comments by grade 7 students provide an interesting point of departure for concluding reflections. One cannot say to what extent these perceptions result from participation in Roman Catholic religious study at Bridge Street School. However, the character, if not the strength, of influence can be surmised: students are led to see Christianity as a religion of love for other persons. Corroboration is furnished by the school administrators' observation that "humanism is the accent" of the program, and also by the comments of two grade 2 teachers. They affirmed that interpersonal values, such as friendship and consideration, are stressed in the Roman Catholic program, much as they are in the subjects of health and social studies.

If, as appears likely, the program is contributing to the students' recognition of love for others as requisite for a Christlike person, it has a warrant for being part of the curriculum. There is in the grade 7 students' perceptions a potential for enrichment which further justifies the program. The concept of selfless love for others, which they appear to have grasped so well, can be made more inclusive and powerful by association with other less frequently mentioned Christian concepts, such as "being like God" (i.e., the Christian conceives of his/her love for people as an imitation, or even an expression, of God's love for all people). Two of the responses among the sixteen classified under "selfless love" did indeed make that association: "learn to love and try to be an image of Jesus and God."

While no Protestant class was polled in the same manner as the grade 7 Roman Catholic class, one can infer from other evidence that Protestant religious study orients students towards love for others. The grade 9 students noted that they "learn about helping people," and, as reported above, the grade 2 teacher felt that it is not enough to know a Bible story about, say, forgiveness – one must be able, through the help of Jesus, to forgive. (It is interesting to speculate whether one of the programs has succeeded more than the other in integrating the concept of love for others with concepts of God and God's relationship with mankind. Exploration of such questions, through discussion among the teachers of the two programs, could be richly rewarding.)

Whatever its content, religious study's impact depends largely, of course, on whether it commands the attention and interest of students. Testimony of teachers and students, and the writer's observations, indicate that it does so at Bridge Street School – which is not to deny instances of student inattention. Religious study is clearly not exempt from the iron law of pedagogy: feed the students' interest with nourishing fare, both familiar and unexpected, or lose the students.

It is apparent that two categories of students benefit from religious study at Bridge Street School: those obtaining religious instruction at home and church receive enrichment and reinforcement from the school program; the other students, who may constitute as much as sixty percent of the religious study enrollment, gain a basic awareness of Christian faith. The evidence also indicated that, partly or wholly as a result of religious study, there is some movement of individuals from the latter to the former category.

If "faith enrichment" and "faith awareness" can be used to denote the major functions of religious study at Bridge Street School, "faith exercise" can perhaps describe the function of the daily recitation of the Lord's Prayer, and of more occasional religious activities, such as those associated with graduation. Students generally seem to recognize the value of prayer as part of the opening exercises, but there may be less satisfaction with the format used for conducting the prayer.

We can only conclude that Bridge Street School provides worthwhile opportunities for the religious development of students. The question remains whether, in so doing, the school is compromising its other functions. What is the evidence in that respect?

One responsibility of a multi-faith public school is to promote or safeguard harmonious relations among students and teachers of different faiths. Once a week, each grade group at Bridge Street School divides to attend separate forms of religious study, or no religious study: does that promote exclusiveness or animosity? No evidence was discovered to that effect. A grade 2 Protestant teacher, two grade 2 Catholic teachers, and a grade 8 Catholic teacher all discounted the hypothesis. Students seem to view attendance at religious study or at the supervised study period simply as routine. The Protestant teacher observed that she never heard any student making an invidious comparison (e.g., "mine's better than yours"). The Protestant coordinator made some analogies – "the fact that we sing about flowers doesn't mean we don't like birds; the fact that you don't like liver doesn't mean you forbid it to others" – and then stated her policy as being not to express an aversion to what others stand for, and not to bar choices (e.g., saying to students that they should never go to such-and-such a church).

The recitation of the Lord's Prayer at the start of each day, and the abstention by a few students, also occasion no resentment. Among the abstaining students are Jehovah's Witnesses and one or more whose religious stance is atheistic. A variety of practical arrangements are resorted to, such as stepping outside the room during the prayer (and, in some cases, during "O Canada" as well), remaining seated, or standing with the others but not joining in the recitation. In every instance, according to the principal and the teachers concerned, the distinctive behavior of the few attracts no criticism, or marked attention, from their classmates. The distinction between the few and the majority with respect to the prayer does not carry over into the rest of school life: all are involved indistinguishably in its activities and friendship groups. There is an exception for some students with respect to participating in Christmas plays, and engaging in certain seasonal activities which many would regard as having a secular character. Thus, a grade 4 child of a Jehovah's Witnesses family was kept home from class events marking Valentine's Day and Halloween. Again, however, the effect is not alienation from the majority. Credit for this is probably owed not only to the students and their families, but also to the sensitivity of the teachers to their wishes and feelings.

The religious study program might be objected to on other grounds than its bearing on inter-faith relations, namely, that it partakes of the functions of the church, whereas the school is a secular institution. There can be no doubt that the program is concerned with faith awareness and faith enrichment, which are certainly objectives sought by the churches. But a clear distinction between those concerns and secular learning does not seem possible or desirable.

That conclusion is supported, for example, by the fact that the whole of the students' life experience – the "secular" as well as the "religious" aspects – is dealt with in the Roman Catholic program. Similarly, in encouraging the students to love other persons by, as the students expressed it, "sharing," "forgiving," "getting along with everyone," the program directly promotes one of the secular objectives of the school. A parallel argument could be based on the content of the Protestant program.

There is another sense in which religious study is, inseparably, both religious and secular. The biblical events and personalities which the students learn about are part of the cultural heritage that the school is expected to transmit. A student ignorant of the Bible, of Moses, the Exodus, the Promised Land, the Nativity, the Crucifixion and Resurrection, to mention only a fraction of the heritage, is as much deprived of secular as of religious development.

Notes

[1] As with the two other cases which are not self-reports by the teacher concerned, the actual name of the school and the identities of the teachers have not been used, thus lessening a possible constraint on data-gathering and the reporting of findings.

[2] Unlike her Roman Catholic counterpart, however, the Protestant co-ordinator feels that the October start is realistic, because volunteers are not always available in September, and the school is heavily involved with other aspects of launching the school year.

[3] Most of the students are not yet able to read the text without much assistance, which has the effect of making the religion lesson a reading lesson as well.

7

A *"Religions of the World" Course for Junior High School Students*[1]

by Sid Bentley with D. Weeren

Is it practical, is it worthwhile, to engage young teenagers in a public school in a serious encounter with world religions? My answer is yes on both counts, in the light of my experiences with an experimental course launched in the early 1970s at William Beagle Junior Secondary School in Surrey, British Columbia. This case study is a brief record of that rich experience – some background, a sketch of approach and content, and the response of students to the course.

Background

My interest in the religions of the world goes back many years, and those were years of personal study. When I made the decision to prepare the world religions elective course, I took a formal course in religions of the west at the University of British Columbia.

My contacts in the varied religious communities of the Lower Mainland are broad. I have cultivated social and intellectual relationships with people in each of the major religions, as well as in some of the more visible sects. The time and effort spent doing this has stood me in good stead over these years. I believe student understanding is more easily attained from interacting with a teacher than from just using a textbook.

Before the course begins, a descriptive letter of permission is sent home with every prospective student. The letter, with a parent's signature of approval, must be returned before the student is allowed to take the course. (The ''no approval'' responses run to about five percent.)

The January, 1984, version of the letter from the school principal read as follows:

To the Grade Nine Parents:

Your son/daughter is enrolled in Social Studies 8 this semester, with Mr. Bentley as a teacher. In this grade only, we have made the Social Studies requirement more flexible.

Mr. Bentley's classes will have a unit on Religions of the World included as supplementary material. The regular material will be covered in the first 3/4 of the course and the World Religions unit will be covered in the last 1/4. Mr. Bentley has taught this material at Beagle for the last ten years.

As noted, your son/daughter is enrolled in Mr. Bentley's Social Studies 8; but if you prefer that they take the regular Socials 8, arrangements will be made to transfer them.

Attached is an explanatory letter about the World Religions unit. This is also a letter of permission, so please sign in the appropriate place so that any necessary changes can be made.

If there are any questions or concerns, please call the school and a teacher will contact you.

The attachment describing the course read in part as follows:

The faiths examined will be Hinduism, Sikhism[2], Buddhism, Judaism, Christianity and Islam.

The time spent on each of the above will be about four hours so there will be limited time for an in-depth study. At the end of each unit a representative of that faith will visit the class. They will not come as lecturers or "evangelists" but as knowledgeable resource people to answer questions in an informal setting.

The central aim of school courses for years has been mastery of a selected amount of content. This is not the intent with Social Studies 8. Each of the faiths will be examined sympathetically to try and understand why it attracts its followers. At no time will the teacher tell a student what he should believe and at no time will the teacher influence the class as to the rightness or wrongness of a belief or an opinion.

This is an experimental course and the teacher makes no claims to being an expert. It will be a parallel learning situation for class and teacher with the teacher maintaining direction, continuity and a timetable.

When I began teaching the course, I looked for a suitable textbook. Every book I found that satisfied my requirements was far too difficult for use as a junior high text. For that reason, I eventually developed my own text, actually an extensive set of mimeographed notes, written by me and edited by an "authority" in each field.

These notes have evolved into a series of teaching guides, under the general title, *Religions of Our Neighbors,* originally published by the British Columbia Ministry of Education in accordance with its policy of providing teachers throughout the province with access to locally developed learning materials. The booklets contained complete scripted lessons for a world religions course offered as an optional segment of the Grade 9 or 10 Social Studies program. Now revised and reissued independently, the series deals with Hinduism, Buddhism, Sikhism, Judaism, Christianity, Islam and, more briefly, with Unitarianism, Zoroastrianism and Baha'i.[3]

Approach and Content

This course is concerned not with religious instruction but rather with religious education. The students are most interested in existential questions such as life and death, good and evil, war and peace, solitude and companionship, and faith and reason. I would like to think the course helps students in their individual searches for meaning at their level and in their own terms.

Each faith is given equal time and equal emphasis. Each unit includes an overview of one religion, its place in history, those people who are naturally associated with it, those doctrinal beliefs that are central or unique to it, its scripture and secondary books, and particular rites and rituals associated with it.

For all religions, I begin with the "myths" or stories. This story form appeals to everyone and the "story" can be comprehended at different levels. I include the Christian "myth" so that the students do not leave with the idea that only "other people" have myths.

The course focuses on living religions. As primary sources, what are better than classroom visits by guests, and student visits to houses of worship? At the end of each unit, a member of the faith that has been studied visits the class to give the students the chance to interact with someone "on the inside." I don't want a lecturer, I want dialogue so I warn the speaker to expect and prepare for lively interaction. Our guests include a Brahmin priest, a Tibetan lama, a Sikh giani, a Jewish rabbi, a Catholic priest, a Protestant minister, a Moslem imam, and a Mormon missionary. In most quarters, I also have a few other speakers representing other sects or faiths. The individual speakers have been selected as much for their ability to interact with the students as for their knowledge. At the end of each course, we take a field trip to Beth Israel Synagogue, Holy Rosary Cathedral, the Khalsa Diwan Sikh Temple, and St. Mary's Ukrainian Orthodox Church. A guide meets us at each place of worship to explain and describe it.

My role as teacher of this course is the result of much thought. I believe I must be willing to explain sympathetically, and without bias, any viewpoint which arises. If possible, each religion should be seen from the point of view of those who belong to it. For this reason, I choose an unusual approach; I take the advocate's position while teaching each religion. This means when I teach Hinduism, "I am a Hindu," when I teach Judaism, "I am a Jew," and so on. From this base, I support and defend each faith. By emphasizing the positive aspects, I try to present each religion in its ideal form. I do not dwell on the "darker pages." Each religion has had its misguided zealots who have done unfortunate things as "representatives" of that faith. In my course, each religion gets equal, positive treatment. Remember, each of these religions is alive and thriving, and affects millions of people's lives *today*.

While preparing the course I wrote some optimistic objectives, and I feel that the course is meeting them. One goal was to make students aware that "we" are not the centre of the universe. Recognition and understanding of ethnic-centred and religion-centred biases, combined with an empathetic sense of common ground, must result in tolerance.

Another goal was to make students aware of the common religious themes of love, sharing, and personal accountability, which, if practised, would result in a better world.

A third goal was to expose students to religious thoughts. A child who grows up with no such exposure has an incomplete framework of reference.

Finally, students must be aware of the effect that religion has on our history – past, present, and future. Without such knowledge, their education is not complete. So my goals for the students were tolerance, responsibility, and a more complete frame of reference.

Those were the content considerations. The practical objectives were, first, a course that would hold the interest of the students and therefore survive as an elective, and second, a course that would be noncontroversial enough to survive in the school system. I believe my course has, to some degree, met all these objectives.

The enterprise is not without risk. Due to the sensitive nature of some of the material, it is important to present an attitude that maintains a balance between defending or justifying the intellectual argument for each religion and safeguarding a student's personal, religious beliefs. This passage, used in explaining the Hindu view of God, illustrates the balance. Christianity, the faith of many of the students, is not disparaged even though its lesser sense of the "absoluteness" of divine law is plainly stated.

It is important that you have an understanding of this God-view that sees God as the impersonal-absolute, the big computer in the sky, the Maker of the rules. These are more than rules, they are laws. These laws are laid down for all. There is no sense of forgiveness. If you break a law, you must accept the consequences. You don't expect to say, "Sorry God, I won't do it again," and God to say, "O.K." That is generally what the Christian believes, since Christianity teaches forgiveness. If you sin, which is breaking the law of God, you go to God and say, "I am sorry; I'll turn my life around; I love you Jesus for giving me this chance for forgiveness; I will sin no more." Jesus will forgive you.

This does not exist in Hinduism, which holds that God makes absolutely immutable laws. The law is the law; if you break the law, you accept the consequences. To explain this difference between a personal and an impersonal God, I'm going to use a story told by a Buddhist (the explanation is also very Hindu).

The Buddhist said that for God to be fair, God must be absolutely impartial. For God to change the rules for some people would be patently unfair. So he drew an interesting analogy. He said, "Let's compare life with going on an automobile journey. First of all, you don't know how to drive a car. You're going to take this trip; so to prepare for the trip, you learn all the rules of the road and all the traffic laws. You are very, very careful and highly disciplined to follow all the traffic laws. This will give you your best chance of completing the trip safely."

Then, cynically, the Buddhist said, "That isn't the way the Christian approaches the trip. The laws are important, but more important is who made the laws. So you research who made the laws and when you find out who wrote the laws, then you make friends with that person and spend all your time telling this person how much you like him or her. Learning what the actual laws are is not really that important." So this particular Buddhist pointed to the Christian emphasis on the lawmaker – loving the lawmaker and appearing to disregard the laws at times, whereas he saw the Buddhist as not being concerned with the lawmaker, because the lawmaker wouldn't change the laws anyway. The secret for the Buddhist was simply to learn the laws and live by them.

This is the idea of immutable law, the karmic law that lays down the consequences for your actions. When you know you've done wrong, you also know that the only hope you have of amending this is to do enough good to compensate for the bad things you've done. You might possibly want to build up a credit balance by doing more good than you have done bad. In that way you would still suffer the consequences of your acts but you would also have earned rewards.[4]

Another source of risk is incompleteness or inaccuracy in the teacher's knowledge of the religions being taught. This is, of course, reduced to the extent that the teacher has studied reliable sources and has communicated with knowledgeable adherents of the religions in question. The direct involvement of such persons as classroom visitors prepared to talk with the students is also a valuable safeguard. Students should not, however, be led to regard either the teacher or the visitor as a complete and infallible source of information about a given religion. The teacher must be secure and honest enough to be able to tell the students at times, "I do not know the answer." Sometimes the teacher will be able to research the answer, but I believe it teaches the students something important about religion (and teachers) if it is acknowledged that there are questions which are beyond answers here and now. Similarly, students need to be made aware that, given human limitations and the diversity of outlooks within each of the world faiths, full protection against conveying erroneous information or impressions is impossible.

The vulnerability to error can be illustrated by reference to the teaching guides mentioned above. Though they had evolved largely through person-to-person contact with knowledgeable adherents of the various faiths, errors in the printed material were identified by spokespersons of those faiths. The spokespersons expressed appreciation of the project, and seemed to recognize that some errors may be an inevitable trade-off for getting basically sound information regarding their respective faiths into the schools. They supplied errata sheets for distribution, with the understanding that the changes would be included in any future editions. In the case of Sikhism, however, the criticism from the local Sikh community was such that the teaching guide was withdrawn from circulation. The text has now been rewritten, accepted by the Sikh community, and reissued.

Response

The test of whether the effort and the risks have been justified is the effect of the course on students. Before discussing student response, it is worth noting that, although over 1,600 students of many faiths have taken the course since its inception over ten years ago, criticisms or complaints from their families have been conspicuous by their absence. In comparison to other courses, parent reaction is unusually frequent and positive. On occasion parents show concern and have questions about the course content (generally at the start of the course), but this is itself a sign of interest rather than of opposition.

Student response can be gauged at various levels, ranging from the informational to the attitudinal to the personal. To begin with the first, it is apparent that students acquire a good deal of knowledge about world religions. An appendix to this chapter contains a test that exemplifies the scope and quantity of information that can be acquired. The scores of the Grade 8 students who wrote the test in January, 1985, indicate that a substantial amount of factual learning occurs. Other things being equal, higher scores could be expected from classes of Grade 9 and 10 students.

While knowledge is worthwhile in its own right, its value is limited. Apart from the fact that we forget the bulk of the information we learn and are tested on at school, knowledge without application is unlikely to retain a place of importance in our stock of facts and concepts. What evidence is there that knowledge gained in the "Religions of the World" course is applied?

There is ample evidence that attitudes towards members of other religious groups improve. Tolerance is increased, prejudice is reduced. The now-retired principal of the school who encouraged the development of the course made this assessment:

> Our goal, to promote understanding and tolerance, has been achieved [I believe to a large extent] by the introduction of the World Religions Course. Racial conflict, which was once quite apparent, has virtually disappeared [from the school] and it would appear that fear and ignorance have been replaced with much more positive attitudes.

A research study[5], using pre- and post-testing and a control group, supported this view by demonstrating significant attitude change.

The nature of the change emerges clearly from student responses on anonymous course evaluation forms. Here is a sampling of replies:

> I think it's shown me that other religions are human too. I had a pretty closed mind before I took the course.
>
> Before, I used to despise people with religion, but now I found out what kind of people they really are.
>
> I used to be prejudiced against Sikhs but now I've learned about them, and they're just practising a religion like everybody else.

Before, I made fun of the Hindus but now I understand why they are the way they are.

Before, when I saw them [Hari Krishnas] I thought *BAD,* but they're not all bad people.

I am a Catholic and I was brought up hating all Jews. Now I like Jews, and Rabbi Segal was a very enjoyable person.

There is less prejudice in me, and I feel happier when I see one of my fellow students in the hallways.

A few students probably retain their previous attitudes notwithstanding the course. For example:

I hate Hindus and it didn't help me learn.

At the third level of impact – personal meaningfulness – the course is harder to assess. The repudiation of prejudice is not the same thing as a conviction that religion has something important to offer to humans. There are indications, nevertheless, particularly in students' essays or their replies to essay-type examination questions, that the knowledge gained in the course is impinging on the religious outlook or quest of at least some students. Here is a sampling of student writing which reveals something of the inner person at work with religious ideas taught or evoked by the course.

Most religion seems to have no proof, except the bible or other ancient scriptures. I believe that God is too far beyond us for us to know what he is, but there are impressions of him around us, in nature and creation and emotion and a lot of other beautiful things. Maybe each religion throws a little light on one piece of God. Maybe God is a force that flows on another level of life and some people have touched that level and seen the answer. Mostly God is something to believe in.

What I learnt about religion was that it doesn't make you a self-centred person. You live for something other than yourself and for your own good. It lets you know there is something after this life, either a life with God or another life in which you can try to be with God or reach the highest of all realms. It teaches you not to fear death then because death can take you to better things.

I learnt that although there are many religions, they mostly believe the same basic things. Religion is a way of finding yourself and if you follow your religion you will find a perfect world. I found that it doesn't matter what religion you are.

In this [course] I learned that most of the religions were very interesting. Whenever a speaker came, they always made me feel as if I wanted to know more about what they would talk about. We are very lucky to take this course because someday in the future, it might come in handy. All of the speakers accepted criticisms very well. I liked to argue with them sometimes, so I can get to know their point of view and vice versa. I like it when religious people stick up for their religion. It sort of makes me happy, because I know I would stick up for mine. I think it is great to have really religious people in this world. Most of them try to expand their religion and try to make people understand the way they do. It means a lot.

I learned that religion is not just going to church and praying to God, but having a full life, enjoyment and pleasure. Many people think that religion is something very mysterious and very blah. But it's something different and unusual that people need.

I learned that religion is a way of life, not just a way to pass a Sunday morning. It is believing in what happens to you after death and living a certain way now in preparation for it.

There are also responses which indicate a sceptical, critical, or hostile attitude towards religious thinking. For example,

If the Jews tried to practice the ethics of brotherhood in the modern world nobody would listen, for in order to succeed today you have to fight your way to the top and that can't be done without hurting people. Just as the saying goes, nice guys finish last.

Religion – I think it is just something people believe in just to live for or just a cheap excuse that people use to explain where we came from – not what really happened – in my opinion. But what you taught me is a belief in something or nothing and to worship it.

Some students with a background of Christian knowledge have found the course helpful in relation to their understanding of Christianity as exemplified by these statements:

What I learnt about Christianity was more details of Jesus' life which I had wondered about. It just cleared the air on what I had already learnt. The best part was clearing up the main three years of Jesus' life even if it was just a rough sketch.

About Christianity, I didn't learn too many new things but I now realize that to become a *real* Christian you cannot break *any* commandments.

The thing I found most interesting or surprising about this faith is the real story on how Jesus was born and if Mary was really a virgin and her marriage status etc. . . . I never knew the real story and I always wondered how it could be possible that Mary was a virgin, but now I'm pretty sure about that story. I also never really understood before about Christ being God and the Son. I never understood about Jesus being the divine and man, but I understand a little better now. I understand why it was important for Him to feel pain and suffer to prove that He was human, then He came back to prove He was divine.

For a few students, the course may be unsettling, as in this instance:

I used to believe that there is a God but now it's hard to say, because if there is only one God, I don't know why there are so many different religions. So now I don't know if there is a God or not.

As with other areas of study, it is difficult for students to make progress in religious awareness and insight if they have to rely solely on a school course. The student whose anonymous response has just been cited needs the opportunity to observe and communicate with persons who have worked through that kind of religious issue. Ideally, the home would provide some of those opportunities, as in these instances, taken from letters written by parents:

> At an age when it appears to be difficult to motivate my teenage daughter . . . , my husband and I were very happy to see her so "turned on" by your course. She enjoyed the trips to churches, temples, etc., but most of all she found the lectures very stimulating, and thought provoking. We enjoyed many dinners at home during that time, in lively discussion.

> I have been a guest speaker in Sid Bentley's world religions class the last couple of years, and he asked me to comment on it to you. I am speaking both as lecturer and parent, for my oldest daughter has taken the course.
> I found that the course offered students of different races and religions an opportunity to explore spiritual concepts without prejudice. I feel this kind of inquiry leads towards not only spiritual maturity, but racial and religious tolerance in the lives of students. My daughter is a believer in Jesus Christ, and all I can say about her is that this course strengthened this faith.

It will be clear from all that has been said that the "Religions of the World" course does not set out to strengthen faith. Its chief object is to promote tolerance among people of different faiths and cultural backgrounds. Yet it does not accomplish that object by making religion seem of only private and incidental importance in life; it does not suggest that the logic of tolerance is: do not discriminate because religion is too insignificant for human beings to deserve being made a basis for discrimination. Rather, the logic of tolerance conveyed is: do not discriminate because religion can be of great significance and worth for human beings – an integral and vital part of their humanness. Given that logic, it is not surprising that some students will emerge from the course with a stronger commitment to their religious faith or, lacking a defined faith, a greater inclination to turn to religion for meaning and value in their lives.

Notes

[1]This chapter is an expanded version of an article with the same title which appeared in *Horizon,* Vol. 19, No. 3, (1980) pp. 22-25.

[2]Although Sikhism is not considered a major faith, it is included because Sikhs are a visible, foreign religious group in our school and community.

[3]A set of ten one-half hour video-taped interviews with practicing members of the various faiths has also been prepared, under the sponsorship of the Pacific Interfaith Citizenship Association of British Columbia. For both the videotapes and the books, inquiries and orders should be sent to: Sid Bentley, Bentley West Publishing Co., #37 2665 Cape Horn Avenue, Coquitlam, B.C., Canada V3K 6B8.

[4]*Hinduism,* Vol. 2 of *Religions of Our Neighbors* (Victoria: Province of British Columbia, Ministry of Education, 1983), pp. 32-34.

[5]The study was conducted by Dr. Kehoe of the University of British Columbia and R. Gallagher of Capilano College.

Appendix

SS8 – Religions Test-Matching Terms

Name: _____

In each question you are given a series of terms which relate to the topic of that question. After each term, in the blank provided, PRINT the letter which is to signify which religion that term relates to.

_____

Letters to be used: B = Buddhism; C = Christianity; H = Hinduism; I = Islam; J = Judaism; S = Sikhism

_____

Each list is arranged alphabetically; some lists will not require some letter(s), some letters might be repeated.

_____

A. Name of God

Allah	_____
Brahma	_____
Jehovah	_____
Jesus	_____
No God	_____
Sat Nam	_____
Vishnu	_____

B. Where Religion founded

Indus River	_____
Jerusalem	_____
Mecca	_____
Nepal	_____
Palestine	_____
Punjab	_____

C. Name of Founder

Abraham	_____
Gautama	_____
Guru Nanak	_____
Jesus	_____
Muhammad	_____
No Founder (?)	_____

D. Name of a great leader

Ali	_____
Gobind	_____
Moses	_____
Paul	_____

E. When founded

No Date	_____
No Date	_____
600 B.C.	_____
0	_____
622 C.E.	_____
1500 A.D.	_____

F. "Bible"

Guru Granth	_____
Koran	_____
New Testament	_____
Torah	_____
Tripitaka	_____
Vedas	_____

G. Language of Bible
   Arabic   _____
   Aramaic   _____
   Gurmukhi   _____
   Hebrew   _____
   Sanskrit   _____

H. How many believers
   600 million   _____
   900 million   _____
   1,000 million   _____

I. Particular dress
   Kepa   _____
   Turban   _____
   Veil   _____

J. Calendar (?)
   B.C.   _____
   C.E.   _____
   A.H.   _____

K. Holydays
   Easter   _____
   Hanukkah   _____
   Shabat   _____
   Yom Kippur   _____

L. Special diets
   Kosher   _____
   No Pork   _____
   Vegetarian   _____
   Milk & Meat   _____

M. Hello
   Namasthe   _____
   Salaam   _____
   Sat Sri Akhal   _____
   Shalom   _____

N. "Priests"
   Gianni   _____
   Guru   _____
   Imam   _____
   Lama   _____
   Rabbi   _____

O. Church
   Ashram   _____
   Dharma Centre   _____
   Gurdwara   _____
   Mosque   _____
   Synagogue   _____

P. Put correct number in blank

Words and numbers
for question "P"

Case containing Prayer, on doorpost	_____	Amrit	– 1
God who decides your next birth	_____	Dharma	– 2
Pilgrimage to Kaaba; once in life	_____	Haj	– 3
Man's duty, given by God	_____	Karma	– 4
Message-story as told by Jesus	_____	Kirpan	– 5
Sugar & water nectar used for baptism	_____	Atma	– 6
Important prayer "Hear O Israel . . ."	_____	Mezuzah	– 7
All your actions, good or bad	_____	Parable	– 8
Feast day when Jesus appeared to disciples	_____	Pentecost	– 9
Word for Soul, in Hinduism	_____	Samsarah	– 10
Orthodox branch of Islam	_____	Sunni	– 11
Short sword worn by baptized Sikhs	_____	Tanach	– 12
God concept in Christianity	_____	Trinity	– 13
Cycles of birth and rebirth	_____	Yama	– 14
Jewish name for "Bible" - (O.T.)	_____	Shema	– 15

Scores

Number of test items: 85

Items answered correctly	Number of students
83	1
82	1
81	1
79	1
76	2
75	2
72	3
71	1
70	2
67	1
66	2
64	4
63	1
62	1
60	3
59	2
58	1
57	1
56	1
55	2
49	1
48	1
45	1
43	1
42	1
41	2
38	1
37	1
36	2
33	1
21	1

Student Total   46

Median Score   61

As a percentage of 85   72%

Epilogue

This book has attempted to demonstrate the value and feasibility of educating religiously in multi-faith schools. The case has been made, and the judgment now rests with you, the reader.

My purpose in adding an epilogue is to allay two concerns which may weigh against a favorable judgment. The first has to do with the completeness of the evidence, the second with the reader's religious convictions.

As is apparent from the "Guide to Further Reading" which follows the Epilogue, there are many voices that deserve a hearing on the subject of this book. Though I might have essayed a comprehensive examination of the viewpoints of a large number of observers in various countries, I judged it more useful to emphasize what is actually being achieved in Canadian schools, while suggesting an interpretive framework within which to place the achievements. The framework, as presented in Chapters 1 and 2, may be summarized as follows: educating religiously is an historically defensible, natural component of schooling, inseparable from secular education, synergetic with moral education, and consistent with students' freedom to learn.

This book's evidence is found mainly in the case studies. They depict three principal modes of educating religiously – through the "secular" curriculum, as exemplified by biblical literature (Chapter 3) and a world religions component in social studies (Chapter 7); through religious observances (Chapter 4); and through religion courses (Chapters 5 and 6). This range might be extended; additional examples of the three modes, drawn from all provinces and territories, could be given, or the five cases that were chosen could be examined in more detail. I would submit, however, that the cases as presented afford educators, parents and the educationally concerned public sufficient evidence that educating religiously in the multi-faith school is a viable undertaking, meaningful for the students concerned.

For schools not currently engaged (other than incidentally) in educating religiously, the cases furnish sufficient grounds for initiating the process. Needless to say, the first step would be a careful consideration of which approach or combination of approaches would best suit the school or system. Insofar as possible, the design should avoid shortcomings that emerge in the case studies, which are not claimed to be flawless models.

As for schools already engaged in one or other form of educating religiously, the case studies can provide both a vindication of their efforts and a stimulus to renewal. For example, a school whose religious education endeavors approximate those of the Bridge Street School (Chapter 6) could consider adopting part or all of the "Religions of the World" course described in Chapter 7, and modifying its opening exercises in the light of the Toronto program (Chapter 4).

95

Yet there may be a hesitancy based on one's own religious convictions. Though willing, and perhaps eager, to advance the religious development of students in multi-faith schools, you may be deterred by a conflict, or apparent conflict, of allegiance. On the one hand, you sense a responsibility to help all students so disposed to deepen their religious awareness. Effectively, that means cultivating religious diversity, through encouraging students to discover the riches of their respective traditions and also to branch out from those traditions as new insights are garnered elsewhere. On the other hand, you also sense the call, based on your own religious commitment, to invite people to the faith or values which you judge to be true. Thus the dilemma arises: how can I be both a promoter of diversity and a convincing witness to the truth as I know it?

I do not suggest that the dilemma can be laid to rest once and for all. If it dies, perhaps that will mean that one or both of the commitments which produce it have died – the commitment to a faith, and the commitment to educating students religiously in a manner consistent with their respective faith traditions. Nevertheless, a response can be made to the dilemma.

It is possible to be deeply committed to one's own faith and to share it with others, while recognizing that much of its profound truth reappears, whether in similar or different form, in other faiths. Openness to other faiths may well be greatest in those with the greatest love for the truth as they have and continue to apprehend it in their own faith. The power of that love reaches out to embrace all that mirrors, illuminates, enlarges what they believe. It is not blind to seeming or real contradictions among faiths, but it is able to keep those contradictions in perspective.

This principle of "commitment with openness" recognizes the dynamic character of religion. If religion were a matter of particular rituals and teachings, established once and for all, it would be foolish to seek enlightenment outside one's own faith. However, religion is not, or should not be, static. The believer is engaged in a journey, a progressive discovery of unimagined truths, a continuous purifying and strengthening of personal integrity and loving kindness. The journey is undertaken in the fellowship of co-religionists, and uses maps and advice handed down by earlier travellers of the same faith; yet it remains an uncharted journey, a journey of faith in, and of love for, what is infinitely greater even than the treasured formulations and customs of the traveller's religious tradition. The believer must be open to all the diverse ways in which the ultimate reality elects to reveal itself and to guide human conduct.

The openness, it must be emphasized, is not an emptiness, for the believer carries the precious endowments of a tradition, the ideas and practices which provide a basis for the discernment and adoption of what needs to be assimilated from other traditions. Religious growth, therefore, involves a deepening of understanding and appreciation of both one's own and others' traditions, a process necessarily mediated by the way in which one apprehends one's own tradition.

Not surprisingly, the purpose of educating religiously in the multi-faith school may be characterized similarly. The process is intended to help students understand and appreciate what they and others believe; this can be accomplished only by respecting and building upon their present lifestance, be it a "religiously orthodox" stance or not.

If the students, in their own way, espouse commitment with openness, they will thank their school for helping them to better understand and enter more wholeheartedly the respective paths they are called to walk in their journey to ultimate fulfillment.

Guide to Further Reading on
Educating Religiously in Multi-Faith Schools

All the works listed shed a useful direct or indirect light on the subject, if only to reveal theoretical or practical obstacles to educating religiously. To facilitate selection, I have specified the aspect(s) of the subject which a particular work illumines, through the following letter-code.

H   Historical background
R   Rationale for and against educating religiously – both general and with respect to particular approaches
O   Observances as a means of educating religiously
F   Formal study of religion as a means of educating religiously
S   "Secular" disciplines as means of educating religiously
D   Developmental considerations – psychological, sociological, pedagogical

The coding, however, goes no further than my familiarity with particular titles permits; therefore, the absence of a letter next to a title does not necessarily mean that the title has nothing significant to offer on the aspect in question.

RO   Colin Alves. *The Christian in Education.* London: SCM Press, 1972.

S   J. Susan Austin. "Religion in Elementary School Social Studies: A Vehicle for Attitudinal Change," *Religious Education.* Vol. 71, September-October, 1976, pp. 474-486.

S   David Barr and Nicholas Piediscalzi, Eds. *The Bible in American Education.* Philadelphia: Fortress Press/Chico, California: Scholars Press, 1982.

O   Gregory Baum. "Reflections on the Lord's Prayer," *Orbit.* Vol. 11, February, 1980, pp. 3-4.

F   Ron Berger. "Look, Friends, It's Just Not Working! Reflections on Religious Studies in the High School," [Alberta Teachers' Association] *Religious Studies and Moral Education Council Newsletter.* Vol. 5, No. 2, January-February, 1979, pp. 5-8.

D   Jerome Berryman, Ed. *Life Maps: Conversations on the Journey of Faith.* Waco, Texas: Word, 1978.

R   Lawrence W. Byrnes. "Guidelines for Teaching About Religion in the Social Sciences." *Elementary School Journal.* May, 1975, pp. 501-505.

R   Calgary Public School Board Committee on Religion in Education. "Religion in Education: Positions, Objectives, Recommendations." Reprinted in: Hugh Stevenson, Robert Stamp, and J. Donald Wilson. *The Best of Times/The Worst of Times.* Toronto: Holt, Rinehart and Winston, 1972, pp. 213-216.

H   A. Stafford Clayton. *Religion and Schooling: A Comparative Study.* Waltham, Mass.: Blaisdell, 1969. 254 pp.

R   W. Owen Cole, Ed. *World Faiths in Education.* London: George Allen and Unwin, 1978.

D   Edwin Cox. *Changing Aims in Religious Education.* London: Routledge and Kegan Paul, 1966.

D   Daniel A. Csanyi. "Faith Development and the Age of Readiness for the Bible," *Religious Education.* Vol. 77, No. 5, September-October, 1982, pp. 518-524.

H   John Dewey. "Religion and Our Schools," *Hibbert Journal.* July, 1908. Reprinted in J. Ratner, Ed. *Intelligence in the Modern World: John Dewey's Philosophy.* New York: Modern Library, 1939, pp. 702-715.

RO   Ecumenical Study Commission. *Opening Exercises: A Policy Statement on Opening Exercises in Ontario Public Schools.* Toronto: Ecumenical Study Commission, 11 Madison Ave., Toronto, M5R 2S2. n.d. 22pp.

R   Ecumenical Study Commission. *Religion in Our Schools: An Ecumenical Reaction to the Keiller Mackay Report.* Toronto: Ecumenical Study Commission. n.d.

R   Murray Elliott. "Religion: An Alternative of Alternatives," in T. Morrison and A. Burton, Eds. *Options: Reforms and Alternatives for Canadian Education.* Toronto: Holt, Rinehart and Winston, 1973, pp. 181-189.

R   David E. Engel. "Objectivity in the Teaching of Religion in Public Schools," *Religious Education.* Vol. 71, January-February, 1976, pp. 81-90.

HRFS "Finding a Place to Stand: New Developments in Religious Education and Their Implications for Ontario Classrooms," theme issue of *Religious Education.* Vol. 73, No. 2, March-April, 1978. pp. 114-247.

D   James W. Fowler. *Stages of Faith: the Psychology of Human Development and the Quest for Meaning.* San Francisco: Harper and Row, 1981.

OF   Kathleen Gibberd. *Teaching Religion in Schools.* London: Longman Group, 1970. pp. 119.

RFD   Thomas H. Groome. *Christian Religious Education.* San Francisco: Harper and Row, 1980.

R   David Hay. "Teaching the Science of the Spirit," in J.G. Priestly, Ed. *Perspectives 9.* Exeter, England: School of Education,

University of Exeter, June, 1982, pp. 37-53.

O   Sid G. Hedges. *With One Voice.* Oxford: Religious Education Press, 1970.

RD   John Hull, Ed. *New Directions in Religious Education.* Barcombe, Lewes, England: The Falmer Press, 1982. 215 pp.

O   John Hull. *School Worship: An Obituary.* London: SCM Press, 1975. 160 pp.

HROF John M. Hull. *Studies in Religion and Education.* Barcombe, Lewes, England: Falmer Press, 1984. 292 pp.

R   Edward Hulmes. *Commitment and Neutrality in Religious Education.* London: Geoffrey Chapman, 1979.

D   Inter-Varsity Christian Fellowship. *International Youth Year.* (Report on Project Teen Canada Survey.) Toronto, IVCF, 1985. (745 Mount Pleasant Road, Toronto, M4S 2N5.)

RF   Robert Jackson, Ed. *Approaching World Religions.* London: John Murray, 1982.

R   M.V.C. Jeffreys. *Truth is Not Neutral.* Oxford: Religious Education Press, 1969. 88 pp.

R   Ernest L. Johns, Ed. *Religious Education Belongs in the Public Schools.* Toronto: Ecumenical Study Commission on Public Education, (11 Madison Avenue, Toronto, M5R 2S2), 1985. 106 pp.

HR   Charles R. Kniker. "Changing Perceptions: Religion in the Public Schools, 1848-1981," *Religious Education.* Vol. 77, No. 3, May-June, 1982, pp. 251-268.

R   Claude Lessard, Roger A. Cormier, Paul Valois, et Louis Toupin. "Les Opinions des Enseignantes et Enseignants du Québec sur le Mode de Regroupement des Commissions Scolaires, la Confessionalité des Écoles et l'Enseignement Moral et Religieux," *Revue des Sciences de l'Éducation.* Vol. VIII, No. 1, 1982, pp. 19-44.

RD   Eric Lord and Charles Bailey, Eds. *A Reader in Religious and Moral Education.* London: SCM Press, 1973.

HR   M.R. Lupul. "Religion and Education in Canada: A Call for an End to Hypocrisy," *Journal of Educational Thought.* Vol. 3, December, 1969, pp. 141-150.

HF   Gerald Rogers McElhiney. "An Investigation into Certain Problems Connected with the Teaching of Religion in the 'Old' City of Halifax."M.A. thesis, Saint Mary's University, Halifax, N.S., 1973.

HR   Tom Malcolm and Harry Fernhout. *Education and the Public Purpose.* Toronto: Curriculum Development Centre, n.d.

R   Ralph Miller. "Is the Religious Alternative School Useful in the Public School System?" *Journal of Educational Thought.* Vol. 16, No. 2, August, 1982, pp. 113-115.

RD   Gabriel Moran. *Religious Education Development.* Minneapolis, Minnesota: Winston Press, 1983. 235 pp.

HO   Penny Moss. "Religious Education and Religious Observance in Toronto Schools," *Orbit.* Vol. 11, No. 1, February, 1980, p. 5.

F   National Conference of Catholic Bishops. *Basic Teachings for Catholic Religious Education.* Washington: Publications Office, United States Catholic Conference, 1973, 36 pp.

R   Nova Scotia. *Report of the Royal Commission on Education, Public Services and Provincial-Municipal Relations.* Halifax: Queen's Printer, 1974, Vol. III, Chapter 41, pp. 101-107 and chapter 54, pp. 25-29.

R   John Richard Neuhaus. "Educational Diversity in Post-Secular America," *Religious Education.* Vol. 77, No. 3, May-June, 1982, pp. 309-320.

R   Ontario. Commission on Religious Education in the Public Schools of Ontario, Keiller Mackay, Chairman. *Religious Information and Moral Development.* Toronto: Ontario Department of Education, 1969. 119 pp.

HRFD   Ouellet, Fernand. *L'Etude des Religions dans les Ecoles.* Waterloo, Ontario: Wilfrid Laurier University Press, 1985. 666 pp.

RFS   N. Piediscalzi and William Collie, Eds. *Teaching About Religion in Public Schools.* Niles, Illinois: Argus Communications, 1977. 258 pp.

HFRS   H.L. Puxley, Ed. "Religious Education in a Pluralistic Society," special edition of *Religious Education.* Vol. 68, No. 4-5, July-August, 1973. 128 pp.

F   Québec, Comité Catholique du Conseil Supérieur de l'Education. *Catholic Religious Instruction and Moral Education in Catholic Schools.* Quebec, 1982. 8 pp.

RF   Québec, Comité Catholique du Conseil Supérieur de l'Education. *Voies et Impasses.* 3 vols. Quebec, 1974.

F   Québec, Ministère de l'Education, Direction de l'Enseignement Protestant. *Elementary School Curriculum. Moral and Religious Education Programme (Protestant),* Level 1 (1981), Level 2 (1981), Level 3 (1982), Level 4 (1982).

F   Québec, Ministère de l'Education, Direction de l'Enseignement Protestant. *Secondary School Curriculum. Moral and Religious Education Programme (Protestant), Secondary 1 (1981), Secondary 2 (1981), Secondary 3 (1981).*

R   Graham M. Rossiter. "The Need for a 'Creative Divorce' between Catechesis and Religious Education in Catholic Schools," *Religious Education.* Vol. 77, No. 1, January-February, 1982, pp. 21-40.

F   Gerard Schmitt. "Teaching Religion in German Secondary Schools," *Religious Education.* Vol. 77, No. 1, January-February, 1982, pp. 88-100.

O   Morris Schumiatcher. "Prayerphobia: Surely the Lord's Prayer Can Only Help Students," *Ontario Education.* Vol. 13, No. 3, May-June,

1981. pp. 26-28.

H C.B. Sissons. *Church and State in Canadian Education.* Toronto: Ryerson Press, 1959.

HR Theodore R. Sizer, Ed. *Religion and Public Education.* New York: Houghton Mifflin, 1967.

HRFSD Ninian Smart and Donald Horder, Eds. *New Movements in Religious Education.* London: Temple Smith, 1975. (Paperback edition, 1978). 271 pp.

R David Stansfield. *The School of Many Colours.* Toronto: Canadian Education Association, 1973. 16 pp.

S Geraldine J. Steensma and Harro W. Van Brummelen. *Shaping School Curriculum: A Biblical View.* Terre Haute, Indiana: Signal, 1977. 178 pp.

RD Merton S. Strommen, Ed. *Research on Religious Development.* New York: Hawthorn Books, 1971. 904 pp.

HRFSD John M. Sutcliffe. *A Dictionary of Religious Education.* London: SCM Press, 1984. 400 pp.

FS Richard Tames. *Approaches to Islam.* London: John Murray, 1982. 264 pp.

R Elmer J. Thiessen. "Indoctrination and Religious Education," *Interchange.* Vol. 15, No. 3, 1984, pp. 27-43. Responses in *Interchange,* Vol. 15, No. 4, 1984, pp. 63-79.

H Robert Ulich. *A History of Religious Education.* New York: New York University Press, 1968. 302 pp.

HRF Michael Warren, Ed. *Sourcebook for Modern Catechetics.* Winona, Minnesota: Saint Mary's Press, 1983. 493 pp.

R Donald Weeren. "Religious and Secular Education: A Dialogue," *McGill Journal of Education.* Vol. 14, No. 2, Spring, 1979, pp. 215-230.

HR John Westerhoff, Ed. *Who Are We?* Birmingham, Alabama: Religious Education Press, 1978.

S Christine Whitaker. "A Survey of the Saskatchewan Division IV English Teachers Concerning the Use of the Bible in the English Curriculum," *Skylark.* Vol. 17, No. 1, Fall, 1980, p. 31.

FS Paul J. Will. "Implementing the Study of Religion in High Schools: One State's Experience," *Religious Education.* Vol. 71, January-February, 1976, pp. 90-95.

R John Wilson. *Education in Religion and the Emotions.* London: Heinemann, 1971. 268 pp.

R John Wren-Lewis. *What Shall We Teach the Children?* London: Constable, 1971. 230 pp.